Things Fall Apart

Things Fall Apart

From the Crash of 2008 to the Great Slump

Ramaa Vasudevan

$SAGE www.sagepublications.com
Los Angeles • London • New Delhi • Singapore • Washington DC

First published in 2013 by

 SAGE Publications India Pvt Ltd
B1/I-1 Mohan Cooperative Industrial Area
Mathura Road, New Delhi 110 044, India
www.sagepub.in

SAGE Publications Inc
2455 Teller Road
Thousand Oaks, California 91320, USA

SAGE Publications Ltd
1 Oliver's Yard, 55 City Road
London EC1Y 1SP, United Kingdom

SAGE Publications Asia-Pacific Pte Ltd
33 Pekin Street
#02-01 Far East Square
Singapore 048763

Published by Vivek Mehra for SAGE Publications India Pvt Ltd, typeset in 11/15 pt Times New Roman by Diligent Typesetter, Delhi and printed at Saurabh Printers Pvt Ltd.

Library of Congress Cataloging-in-Publication Data Available.

ISBN: 978-81-321-1098-9 (HB)

The SAGE Team: Rudra Narayan, Shreya Lall, Nand Kumar Jha, and Rajinder Kaur

For Subba and Sudesh

Contents

Figures

Abbreviations

ABS	asset-backed security
AIG	American International Group
AIGFP	The AIG Financial Products
CDO	collateralized debt obligation
EBRD	European Bank for Reconstruction and Development
ECB	European Central Bank
EFSF	European Financial Stability Facility
ESM	European Stability Mechanism
FDIC	Federal Deposit Insurance Corporation
FSMA	Financial Services Modernization Act
GDP	gross domestic product
GSTC	Goldman Sachs Trading Corporation
ISDA	International Swaps and Derivatives Association
IMF	International Monetary Fund
LIBOR	London Interbank Offered Rate
LTCM	Long-Term Capital Management

MBS   mortgage-backed security

MLEC   Master Liquidity Enhancement Conduit

PASOK   Panhellenic Socialist Movement

SEC   Security Exchange Commission

SPV   Special Purpose Vehicle

TARP   Troubled Asset Relief Program

Preface

This book is meant for anyone who is interested in understanding the structural roots and continuing consequences of the crisis set in motion by the crash of financial markets in 2008. The literature on the crisis is huge and expanding, and this book offers, I hope, an accessible gateway to exploring this vast literature. The writing of this book has been shaped and enriched by many friendships and I have incurred more debts in the process than I could possibly enumerate.

The seed of this book was, in a sense, sown years before the collapse of Lehman and in fact years before I came to the United States. My engagement with the theories of capitalist crisis began in the 1990s, when among a host of other issues, the imminent crisis of capitalism was the subject of heated and passionate debates with friends in India. I cannot even begin to name the people or chronicle the deep impact these debates had when I was trying to make sense of the crisis that unfolded more than a decade later. I hope that all those friends will find something of value in this book.

This book is dedicated to C.V. Subba Rao and Sudesh Vaid, friends and mentors, who shaped and nurtured my intellectual and political development. My deepest regret is that they are not alive to read this book.

Duncan Foley played a critical role in the development of my understanding of dollar hegemony and the international monetary system. My profound intellectual debt to him, however, goes far beyond that. Anwar Shaikh and his long-standing engagement with capitalist dynamics and crisis has been a source of inspiration. Gerard Dumenil, whose work (with Dominique Levy) on the crisis blends a rich statistical and historical account with a penetrating analytical perspective, has also shaped the perspective of the book in profound ways.

It was wonderful to have Deepankar Basu as a colleague and friend during the dramatic events of the 2008 Crash and be able to talk through what was happening on practically a daily basis. I am especially grateful to Shailaja Fennel without whom the book would never have got written! Shailaja also read and critically commented on the first draft.

The data presented in the book is only a very basic rudimentary and broad-brush empirical picture, and I have drawn from the rigorous research of other economists and scholars. Ariel Resheff and Thomas Phillipe generously passed on their data on banking wages. Hyun S. Shin was extremely helpful and pointed me in the right direction for data on the rise of the broker-dealer. Emmanuel Saez and Thomas Piketty's seminal dataset on income inequality (available on Saez's website) was an invaluable resource.

In the accounts of the unfolding events I have drawn rather extensively, and in more ways that I have been able to adequately acknowledge, from the in-depth reporting and analysis in newspapers, the business press and magazines; in particular the *New York Times*, the *Financial Times*, the *Atlantic, Mother Jones, Dollars and Sense*, and the *Economist*, as well as the wonderfully insightful blogs—Naked Capitalism Baseline Scenario and FT Alphaville. I have presented the argument about the role and interconnections between financialization and dollar hegemony in writings in the *Monthly Review, Review of Radical Political Economics*, and the *Economic and Political Weekly*. A special thanks to Nagraj Adve who read through the draft manuscript with painstaking precision, pointing out the numerous places where the arguments were opaque, forcing greater clarity. Sammy Zahran also provided valuable feedback on some chapters.

Without the affection and support of friends—in the United States and back in India—and family—by birth and marriage—this book would have been impossible to write. My husband, Ashok, shared the journey though all the rough patches and moments of discovery, while pulling off the impossible feat of being both unfailingly encouraging about the project and ruthlessly critical while reading through the manuscript!

Chapter 1

All That Is Solid Melts into Air

If risk is properly dispersed, shocks to the overall economic system will be better absorbed and less likely to create cascading failures that could threaten financial stability. The broad success of that paradigm seemed to be most evident in the United States over the past two and one-half years … This favorable turn of events has doubtless been materially assisted by the recent financial innovations that have afforded lenders the opportunity to become considerably more diversified and borrowers to become far less dependent on specific institutions or markets for funds.

— A. Greenspan, remarks before the Council on Foreign Relations, Washington, DC, November 19, 2002

… the low-inflation era of the past two decades has seen not only significant improvements in economic growth and productivity but also a marked *reduction* in economic volatility, both in the United States and abroad, a phenomenon that has been dubbed "the Great Moderation." Recessions have become less frequent and milder, and quarter-to-quarter volatility in output and employment has declined significantly as well.

— B. Bernanke, remarks at Federal Reserve Bank of St Louis, St Louis, Missouri, October 8, 2004

In advanced economies, deep recessions have virtually disappeared in the Post World War II period.

— IMF World Economic Outlook, October 2007, p. 173

Blue Ridge Corporation was an investment trust launched with much fanfare in the month of August. One of its attractions was that it allowed investors to swap their portfolio of unwanted stocks for the better-valued stock of this trust. The bulk of the common shares of Blue Ridge Corporation were, in turn, owned by Shenandoah Corporation, a newly minted investment trust set up barely a month earlier by Goldman Sachs Trading Corporation (GSTC). GSTC marked the first foray of Goldman Sachs into the thriving business of investment trusts about seven months earlier. The investment bank had sponsored the trading corporation with an initial issue of a million shares at US$10 a share. In a booming market, the trust sold 90 percent of these shares to the public at US$104. Within months the shares had doubled in value, prodded in part by purchases by the trading corporation itself. Goldman Sachs was able to, through this Russian doll structure of investment trusts that sponsored investment trusts, transform its initial 10 percent stake in the GSTC into ever larger pools of capital.

As long as stock prices were rising, the pyramid of trusts reaped huge dividends and the stock of these trusts was lapped up by eager investors, secure in their belief that the investment trusts were privy to knowledge denied to the ordinary investors and could ceaselessly yield returns on their behalf. The investor could borrow from the banks and brokerages that sponsored these trusts, simply by posting these securities as collateral along with a small margin of cash. Such trading on the "margin" allowed the investors to reap the returns of rising prices in a booming stock market by putting up a small portion of the purchase price. In the single month of August, Goldman Sachs issued securities worth more than US$250 million.[1]

The year was 1929.

It was the peak of the stock market boom of the 1920s, and investment trusts were popping up at the rate of one every business day. The value of the stock of GSTC rose to a high of nearly US\$326.[2] It was of this spectacular promotion by Goldman Sachs that John Kenneth Galbraith wrote, "It is difficult not to marvel at the imagination which was implicit in this gargantuan insanity. If there must be madness, something may be said for having it on a heroic scale."[3]

The extent of madness became evident when the value of the GSTC fell to US\$1.75 after the stock market bubble burst in fall of 1929. The collapse in stock prices during the Crash of 1929 led to spiraling effects through the pyramid of investment trusts, bringing down the trading corporation. As stock prices fell, the loans that had funded the margin trades were called in. The frenzy of selling that ensued brought down prices even more precipitously, ruining many who had hoped to make their fortunes out of nothing.[4]

Walter Sachs, one of the Sachs brothers heading the bank at the time, when asked what prompted this frenzied promotion is said to have replied, "I confess to the fact that we were all influenced by greed. We were carried away by the bull market, we thought these values were going to be justified ... and the bottom fell out of everything and we were caught with our pants down."[5]

Eight decades later, remarkably similar feats of financial ingenuity and unbridled greed have brought about a collapse of financial markets and the prospect of a long slump. Shadowy banking structures and the mad and dizzy rush of massive trades in obscure financial products anointed as quality investment by the high priests of finance, fuelled the housing bubble and the aggressive pursuit of questionable loans in the subprime markets.

The Crash of 2008, when financial markets came to a standstill in the wake of the collapse of Lehman in September, brought this orgy of speculation to a halt. Then, as now, Goldman Sachs has come to symbolize the worst excesses of speculative manias. But in a far cry from the rueful admission of culpability by Walter Sachs, the current head of Goldman Sachs when testifying before the Financial Inquiry Commission investigating the causes of the Crash likened it to the risks of a freak season where four hurricanes hit the East Coast in a single summer. Unimpressed at this attempt to disavow responsibility, the head of the commission Phil Angelides is said to have retorted, "Acts of God are exempt. These were acts of men and women."

As we look back at the causes and contemplate the impact of the Crash of 2008, it is difficult to swallow the logic that this is the result of a random fluke event—an aberration in the otherwise steady clip of innovation and growth. We have after all been here before. Chances are we will find ourselves back here again.

A tempting narrative is one that hones in on the criminal greed and hubris of a few key players or individuals. The Gilded Age before the Crash of 1929 was the arena where Charles Ponzi ran his notorious swindle. But when the Pecora Commission investigated in 1932 the causes of the stock market bubble, it was "respected" personages like Charles Mitchell, the head of National City Bank, the precursor to Citibank, Albert Wiggins, the president of Chase National Bank and J.P. Morgan Jr., the head of J.P. Morgan bank, who were called in. Mitchell had aggressively pushed the sales of stocks and securities moving into riskier and riskier territory while disregarding the bank's own negative evaluations. In the wake of the Crash, he cornered bonus worth around US$1 million but managed to evade taxes by selling the stock (which was actually pledged against a loan to J.P. Morgan) at a loss to his wife. Wiggins was found short selling the stock of his own bank—that

4

is, selling borrowed stock with the intention of returning the loan after buying the stock at lower prices in the future.[6]

The Crash was, however, more than the outcome of the excesses of few key players. The focus on the actions of individuals obscures the extent to which these practices were endemic to the entire class of financiers, and to the system itself.

Another narrative ascribes the leading role to the state. Lax monetary policy that opened the floodgates of cheap money has also been blamed for stoking the speculative fires. The easing of monetary policy by the US Federal Reserve board between 1925 and 1928, in an attempt to stem the influx of gold to the United States after Britain restored the gold standard at the prewar exchange rates, has been ascribed a lead role in the explanation of why the stock market boom got out of control.[7] A permissive policy environment and the lax regulatory framework have also been regarded as critical to enabling the flourishing of speculative activity. One of the responses to the Great Depression was the institution of a regulatory framework to rein in these speculative tendencies. The deeper underlying forces that gave rise to the bull rush of the 1920s have not been wiped out, but merely held in abeyance.

The steady erosion of the regulatory mechanism that distorted incentives and provided a fertile ground for the proliferation of finance is, however, a consequence of the rising power of financial and corporate capital. While such policies, like the deregulation, give free rein to the unstable dynamics of finance, the tendency toward taking on more risk is inherent to the way financial markets and players function. The tendency to generate increasing fragility—the cycles of booms and busts—is endemic to finance. The history of capitalism is dotted with "manias, panics and crashes."[8] In the past three decades alone, the United States has gone through the savings and loan crisis in the 1980s, the dot-com boom in the 1990s and most recently the housing boom that was the prelude to the Crash.

A buoyant sense of optimism, even complacency, had prevailed in the years before the crisis. Despite the evidence of booms and busts which should have warned "against accepting a period of relative tranquility in a capitalist economy as anything other than a lull before the storm,"[9] there was a dominant sense among those at the helm of policy, in advanced capitalist countries and United States in particular, that the instabilities of capitalism had been tamed by the innovations in finance. Similar "hope and optimism" had marked the years before the stock market crash. Andrew Mellon, the Secretary of the US Treasury, had reassured the markets in the fall of 1928 that, "there is no cause for worry. The high tide of prosperity will continue."[10]

In the aftermath of the crisis, there has been some soul searching within the economics profession, in particular, of how the discipline became so out of touch with things.[11] The Queen of England, while visiting the London School after the fall of Lehman, famously asked why no one saw the crunch coming. In a letter on behalf of the British academy, a bunch of economists responded that this failure "was principally a failure of the collective imagination of many bright people, both in this country and internationally, to understand the risks to the system as a whole."[12]

It is, of course, not true that there were no voices of dissent.[13] There were enough economists (including Steve Keen,[14] Dean Baker,[15] Wyne Godley,[16] Nouriel Roubini,[17] Paul Krugman,[18] and Joseph Stiglitz to name just a few) who had warned of the building fragility. There is enough in both the margins and the cutting edge of economic theory that offers insights into how the markets can run amok. In the heady euphoria of the boom years such voices were unwelcome. The profession imposes a powerful incentive to conformity. The purveyors of ideas and theory are hardly immune to the problems of "cognitive capture" or blatant conflicts of interests.[19] The pervasive influence of a narrow and myopic worldview of the "efficacy of market forces" did play its part in shaping policy responses and giving intellectual sanction to the booming business of finance, but it is also a product of the larger social structure.

To understand the roots of this Crash of 2008, it is not enough to focus on the criminal swindles perpetuated by Bernie Madoff and Allen Stanford, or even the more rampant risky practices that had become the norm with the major banks such as Citibank and Goldman Sachs. It is also not enough to decry the failure of policy to curb unbridled risk taking with other people's money, or the failure of policy makers and economists to see the signs of the inevitable collapse.

The Crash has now given way to the Great Slump—a long and protracted contraction of the US economy. We need to penetrate the fog of finance and explore the structure and balance of class forces that constitute this system and engage with the systemic forces that propel the dominant role of finance and its propensity to runaway speculation. Finance is integral to the functioning of the capitalist economic system. It also magnifies and accelerates the impact of disruptions that arise from weaknesses and fissures of this system. The Great Slump is a manifestation of a deeper structural crisis.

Such systemic crises have punctuated the turbulent trajectory of the growth of capitalism. The Crash of 1929 heralded the onset of the Great Depression. Before the Great Depression of the interwar years there was the Long Depression that set in the 1870s. Between the Great Depression and the current crisis we had the stagflation of the 1970s with a long spell of rising unemployment and inflation.

The fact that crises are a recurrent phenomenon does not imply that each crisis is exactly the same. Every crisis is characterized by distinct, historically contingent features. Just as the lessons of history have a bearing on how we understand and respond to the current crisis, there is something to be learned from exploring the specificities of the current crisis. The analytical tradition of Marx, Keynes, and Minsky, in particular, offers insights into the roots of this crisis, and there is already a rich body of literature that investigates the roots of the crisis from this perspective.[20]

In a way, the seeds of the present crisis were sown as capitalism responded to the structural crisis of the 1970s. The rise to dominance of finance reflected a structural transformation that engineered a revival of profitability and investment by systematically appropriating a greater share of the earnings of the working poor. This rise reflects the increasing social and political power of financial and corporate capital and the managerial executive class. This realignment was fostered by the neoliberal backlash against state interventions that impeded the pursuit of profits. Neoliberalism is in essence the ideological basis of the drive to give a free rein to market forces and corporate power. It also led to the weakening of social safety nets and protections to the working poor. The neoliberal phase as a consequence witnessed a sharp exacerbation of inequality.

The revival of profits also hinged on the ability of US financial and corporate capital to weld the global economy into a tightly integrated circuit of capital accumulation through a global network of production. The United States, in the past two decades, has developed a tremendous appetite for imports, in particular for primary commodities and cheap manufactures, and the off-shoring of manufacture has facilitated the squeeze on workers domestically.

The privileged role of the dollar in the international financial system accorded to the United States an unrivalled access to global surpluses. The US deficits which have been growing since the 1980s kept the global economy awash in dollars even as its capital markets drew and recycled funds from around the world. The proliferation of financial flows, spearheaded by US financial and corporate capital, was linked to the preservation of the hegemony of the dollar. A critical part of the responses to the crisis of the 1970s has been the establishment of this hegemony in global financial markets after the Bretton Woods arrangements set up after the Second World War collapsed and the gold standard was abandoned in 1971. The roots of the current crisis are embedded in the structure of dollar dominance that has evolved since the 1970s. The crisis is as much a crisis of the neoliberal model of accumulation that finance launched as it is of the mechanism by which dollar hegemony was preserved.

For the past three decades, the recourse to debt has boosted consumption in the United States despite stagnant wages, and the depth and breadth of the US financial markets attracted funds from the rest of the world despite the growing deficits and debt. This process appeared to be self-sustaining. The fault lines of this phase of capitalist dynamics were, however, developing along growing income polarization and growing global imbalances. In the last decade, predatory loans to low-income households in the United States became the fodder for the surging earnings of finance.

The collapse of the housing market was the catalyst that set the events of the fall of 2008 in motion. The systemic crisis that unfolded in the aftermath of the Crash touches not just the big banks and Wall Street but more urgently ordinary lives across the globe.

Understanding why it happened is the first step to evolving a long-term response. This book is written with the conviction that such understanding needs to go beyond the confines of those engaged with high theory or high policy.

The book begins with a brief account of the dramatic events that marked the collapse of the financial markets in 2008 (Chapter 2). It places these events in the context of the evolution of the financial system and the proliferation of complex and opaque financial securities in the next chapter (Chapter 3). Chapter 4 explores the response of the US state to the unfolding crisis and highlights how the cosy nexus between the finance and the state constrained and shaped the response of the state. Chapter 5 traces the realignment of class forces and the changing structure of the US economy over the past three decades that were integral to the rise to dominance of finance and the growing polarization of the US economy. This rise is entwined in the fashioning of the globally integrated circuit of production, accumulation and capital flows, and the hegemony that the dollar enjoys as international money. Chapter 6 explores the means by which this hegemony was established and extended. Chapter 7 explores how the collapse of financial markets in the United States triggered a profound crisis for the Eurozone and the implications for the continued dominance of the dollar internationally. The final chapter outlines the contours of the contradictions that would shape the evolving outcome of the crisis.

Chapter 2

The Tip of the Iceberg

After all, you only find out who is swimming naked when the tide goes out.

— Warren Buffett, letter to shareholders of Berkshire Hathaway,
February 28, 2002

Between September 8 and September 16 of 2008—a period of a little over a week—US financial markets were gripped by a maelstrom that threatened to decimate its very foundations. In eight tumultuous days, the United States saw the nationalization of two giants of America's mortgage markets with assets of US$1.8 trillion, the disappearance of two of the world's biggest investment banks, with combined assets of US$1.5 trillion, and the rescue of what was once the world's biggest insurer, with assets of about US$1 trillion.[1] The financial landscape seemed to be irrevocably transformed in those eight days. These events were just the tip of the iceberg.

The crisis had its origins in a US real estate bubble fueled by easy money and lax lending standards that seduced countless Americans into sinking deeper and deeper into debt. The rumblings of trouble were evident the previous summer as rising foreclosures and defaults on the loans to the poorest and least credit worthy borrowers—the subprime mortgages—broke the dizzying spell. The mortgage industry practice became increasingly suspect, and one of the most aggressive mortgage lenders in the United States, Countrywide Financial, suddenly saw its credit machine grind to a halt, raising fears that the global liquidity crisis was worsening. The money markets where banks lent to each other overnight to cover their daily operations went into a tailspin and banks started charging punitive rates for these loans. There was a sharp spike in interest rates in Europe triggered by the announcement by the French bank BNP Paribas of a suspension of three of its funds. The doubts burst into the open on August 9 when central banks in Europe and North America were forced to inject more than US$100 billion into the overnight money markets in order to quell the panic. The meltdown was just beginning.[2]

The first shock wave of the unfolding crisis, however, struck in the United Kingdom and not in the United States.

THE ROCKY START

On September 14, 2007, the offices of Northern Rock, the fifth biggest mortgage lender in Britain, were besieged by long queues as depositors scrambled to pull out their money. Nearly a million pounds were withdrawn in a single day. This was the first bank run in England in more than one and a half centuries. The last time England witnessed such a bank run was in 1866 when Overend, Gurney and Co., a leading discount house and a "banker's bank," second only to Bank of England, suspended payments. The panic which spread across London, Liverpool, Manchester, Norwich, Derby, and Bristol following this announcement, with large crowds around Overend Gurney's head offices, almost brought London's banking system down.[3]

Overend and Gurney were steeped in the nineteenth century financial revolution—transforming short-term deposits into working capital to finance the building of ships, shipyards, and railroads. More than a century later Northern Rock was involved in the mortgage business, actively orchestrating loans of more than 100 percent of the value of properties to first-time buyers and grabbing an increasing chunk of the mortgage market. Its net residential lending had risen by 55 percent in the first eight months of 2007. Northern Rock was also fairly aggressive in moving from the traditional funding of its operations with retail deposits to a greater resort to wholesale markets for cash. By the summer of 2007, only 23 percent of its liabilities were in the form of retail deposits of about 1.5 million savers.[4] The remaining funding came from short-term borrowing in the capital markets.

With the drying up of the capital markets in the summer of 2007 and the plunging of its share prices, Northern Rock began to find it increasingly difficult to secure funding. After talks with several potential buyers failed, including Lloyds TSB, Northern Rock was forced to turn to the Bank of England. Finally, on September 14, Mervyn King, the governor of the Bank of England, announced emergency support lending to the bank. The announcement triggered a panic. Northern Rock's share price dropped 30 percent in a single day. The run on the stricken Northern Rock continued until the Bank of England undertook an unconventional move of offering loans against riskier collateral, including mortgages, and Alistair Darling, the Chancellor of the Exchequer, gave a taxpayer-backed guarantee on all the existing deposits.

When Northern Rock found that it was unable to fulfill its obligations to repay the loan from the Bank of England by the February deadline, a new plan was worked out with advisors from Goldman Sachs (who were of course paid for their services from taxpayer's money!). Hopes were now pinned on wangling a private sector deal to sell off Northern Rock's debt. The Goldman Sachs scheme replaced the original Bank of England loan and Treasury indemnity with a bond issue that would be guaranteed by the Treasury. When Olivant, the private equity group, dropped out, the Virgin consortium and a rival, proposal from Northern Rock's board of directors, became the two main contenders for the sale. When these deals fell through, Alastair Darling unveiled a new plan for nationalizing the beleaguered bank (again with the blessings of Goldman Sachs) in February 2008.

The first domino had fallen.

EMBRACING THE BEAR

The next strike was Bear Stearns, an 85-year-old institution and the fifth largest investment bank in the United States. Bears Stearns was a major prime broker, providing funding and back up for hedge funds. It was also one of the biggest traders in mortgage-backed securities (MBSs).[5] In the spring of 2007, Bear Stearns was trading at around US$150 a share. That summer two of its hedge funds that had bet heavily on subprime loans—High-Grade Structured Credit Strategies Master Fund and the smaller High-Grade Structured Credit Strategies Enhanced Leverage Master Fund— imploded. The first had borrowed, or "leveraged," as much as 35 times its available money to trade, and the second an astounding 100 times its cash. An audacious plan to preempt disaster by launching a new company Everquest Financial (stuffed with the assets of the battered hedge funds) and pawning off the risky assets to retail investors, backfired. When big lenders such as Merrill Lynch and JPMorgan Chase were threatening to seize their collateral, Bear Stearns was forced to pledge about US$3 billion to bailout these hedge funds but could not stem the collapse. The write-downs of its assets continued and various attempts to broker deals with potential investors fell through. James Cayne, the CEO, resigned in January and appointed a new successor Alan Schwartz.

On March 10, 2008, the share price of Bear Stearns went into a free fall as rumors of insolvency gathered momentum. The irony is that the firm was sitting on US$18 billion in cash reserves. As the panic brewed, the Federal Reserve (acting with the European Central Bank [ECB], Bank of Canada, and the Swiss National Bank [SNB]) announced a novel new securities-lending program of US$200 billion for major Wall Street banks that would take off the illiquid mortgages from the balance sheets of banks and securities firms in exchange for more liquid Treasury securities. The move, which did help most financial stocks rebound, was interpreted as an effort directed mainly at saving Bear Stearns—which continued to be perceived as vulnerable. Firms wanting to get rid of the "risky" Bear Stearns instruments sought to sell these to third parties. Goldman Sachs, Credit Suisse, and Deutsche Bank were flooded with novation letters. These novations were requests to these banks to step in and replace Bear Stearns (now perceived to be dodgy) as the other party to their contracts. When Credit Suisse and Goldman Sachs stopped accepting these novation requests, the money began to dry up as overnight lenders began withdrawing and demanding cash for outstanding loans.

On March 13, the Federal Reserve and the Treasury were informed that Bear Stearns might be forced to file for bankruptcy protection the following day. The recent fiasco of Northern Rock across the Atlantic underlined the imperative for decisive action. The fact that Bear Stearns was one of the primary dealers on which

Wall Street banks and the Federal Reserve relied to smoothen the day-to-day workings of the financial system raised the stakes.

The Federal Reserve moved on March 14 to provide temporary emergency financing to Bear Stearns. This was affected through a 28-day direct credit line of an undisclosed amount to JPMorgan Chase, for the purpose of relending to Bear Stearns. This move was a radical departure from conventional lending practice. In the normal course, investment banks were not eligible to borrow from the discount window of the Federal Reserve. This arrangement gave Bear Stearns access to the "discount window" by lending to J.P. Morgan, and allowing the bank to act as a funnel through which the Fed could channel funds into Bear's vaults.

The fire sale continued, resulting in a 47 percent drop in the company's share price, wiping out billions of dollars in market value. The investment bank teetered on the brink of bankruptcy. The Fed and the Treasury decided to push for a buyout that would be completed by the evening of March 16, before Asian markets opened for trading. The Bear Sterns executives who had believed they had 28 days to negotiate a buyout were now in a frantic rush to broker a deal over the weekend. After intense negotiations between J.P. Morgan and Bear Stearns executives, Treasury Secretary Henry Paulson Jr., Fed Chairman Ben Bernanke, and New York Federal Reserve Bank President Timothy Geithner, the Federal Reserve agreed to back up to US$30 billion of losses from a deal where JPMorgan Chase would take over the troubled company at a mere US$2 a share. The stock had been worth US$70 a week before. The story is that James Dimon the head of J.P. Morgan had been considering a price between US$4 and US$8 but was told by Treasury Secretary Paulson not to go above US$2. Under the terms of the acquisition, J.P. Morgan would buy Bear Stearns for about US$236 million in total.[6] According to market share value, it had been worth approximately US$20 billion in January 2007 and US$3.5 billion as recently as March 14.

On the same day that the takeover of Bear Stearns was announced the Fed also announced that it was widening the access to the Fed's discount window that was traditionally reserved for commercial banks to nonbanking financial institutions, including investment banks. Now big Wall Street firms could go directly to the Fed for emergency loans, a privilege reserved until now to commercial banks that were under the ambit of the regulatory oversight of the Fed. The Fed also again lowered the discount rate, which it had recently cut by three-quarters of a percentage point, to 2.5 percent from 3.25 percent.

After stormy meetings with Bear Stearns stockholders, the sale price was raised to US$10 a share from US$2. The new deal was that J.P. Morgan would cover the first US$1 billion in losses if the value of Bear Stearns' securities fell, with the Federal Reserve responsible for losses beyond that up to US$29 billion. J.P. Morgan came out well from the deal, acquiring Bear Stearns' coveted prime brokerage business, at a rock bottom price and negligible risk because most of the burden of risk was taken on by the Federal Reserve.[7] A historical analogy is the banking panic of 1907, which was resolved by J.P. Morgan stepping forward to restore confidence—just as Jamie Dimon, his successor as the bank's chief executive did a century later.

Bear Stearns was saved from bankruptcy by this last minute rescue, but there is an irony in that a decade earlier, in 1998, when the troubled hedge fund, Long-Term Capital Management (LTCM) collapsed, triggering fears of a global financial meltdown, Bear Stearns, the smallest, most freewheeling of Wall Street investment banks, refused to join the syndicate of Wall Street firms that bailed it out.

Many Bear Stearns executives see the demise of Bear Stearns as the result of a predatory raid—a systematic assault by rumor. In their depositions to the Security Exchange Commission (SEC), they have pointed to two hedge funds, Chicago-based Citadel and SAC Capital Partners of Stamford, Connecticut, and also to their main competitor Goldman Sachs as the chief orchestrators of the fall. The holding action orchestrated by the Federal–Treasury combine and J.P. Morgan could not stem the tide. By the summer of 2008, it was quite clear that the financial system was witnessing an unraveling of far-reaching consequences.

THE SUMMER OF 2008

On July 1, Countrywide Financial, the largest mortgage seller in the United States, was acquired by Bank of America (one of the largest commercial banks in the United States).

Countrywide Financial Corporation had been started in New York nearly four decades ago by Angelo R. Mozilo, a butcher's son from the Bronx, and David Loeb, a founder of a mortgage banking firm in New York. By 2007 it had ridden on the crest of the housing boom to transform itself into a US$500 billion mortgage company with 62,000 employees, 900 offices, and assets of US$200 billion. Countrywide's entire operation and incentive pay structure were intended to wring maximum profits out of the mortgage-lending boom. It actively fostered the pursuit of questionable loans with enormous fees. Subprime loans were about 8.7 percent of the US$470 billion in loans that Countrywide made in 2006. Countrywide's margins on these loans, which imposed heavy costs on borrowers, were as high as 15 percent of the loan.[8]

18

Then in June 2007, the company made the stark announcement that the rate of foreclosure had doubled in the first five months of that year. Almost one in four subprime loans that Countrywide services was delinquent. The announcement sparked a panic and Countrywide found itself unable to sell or borrow in the commercial paper market, one of its traditional sources of liquidity. By August 2007, the company was forced to completely draw down its US$11.5 billion credit line from a consortium of 40 banks.[9] Later that month, Bank of America invested US$2 billion in shares that were convertible to common voting stock amounting to a 16 percent stake in Countrywide. This development fueled speculations that Countrywide had become a takeover target. In January 2008, Bank of America announced that it had agreed to pay about US$4 billion in stock to acquire Countrywide with the hopes that the deal would bolster Bank of America's position in the mortgage market while rescuing Countrywide from possible bankruptcy.

Fresh travails afflicted Countrywide as the United States Trustee Program (part of the US justice department) filed a lawsuit at the end of February against Countrywide, and Illinois sued Countrywide in June for defrauding borrowers by selling them costly and faulty loans. Other states quickly followed suit. When Bank of America finally took over Countrywide on July 1, the value of the acquisition, because the price of shares had dropped, was now US$2.8 billion.

Angelo Mozilo, the ex-CEO of Countrywide, left the company an immensely rich man. He was not a big buyer of Countrywide stock but had generous stock options which he sold at huge profits. Since the time the company listed its shares on the New York Stock Exchange in 1984, he is reputed to have made US$406 million selling Countrywide stock. As the subprime mortgage collapse began to unfold in 2007, he went on a selling spree making

19

US$129 million from stock sales in 12 months—about one-third of the entire amount he had garnered over the previous 23 years.[10] Mozillo faces charges of insider trading and fraud, which he settled for the payment of US$67.5 million (about a third of which will be paid by Bank of America which took over Countrywide).

IndyMac Bancorp, an offshoot of Countrywide Financial, was the next to fall. This California-based bank with assets of US$32 billion is one of the biggest savings—or thrift—banks to fail in US history. It specialized in making and selling so-called Alt-A mortgage loans. These loans were provided to customers more credit worthy than subprime borrowers but who did not qualify for a prime rate loan.

In June 2008, a letter from Charles Schumer, the New York senator, expressing concerns about the bank's viability was released. The firms already in a precarious financial position saw its hopes of finding a buyer or procuring an infusion of cash evaporate. This was despite the dodgy attempt by Office of Thrift Supervision to help it bolster its "financial position" by backdating US$18 million of a US$50 million capital infusion that occurred on May 9 (in the second quarter) to the first quarter. The backdating meant that IndyMac's financial position could be recorded as being above 10 percent, the threshold that demarcated the "well capitalized" from the merely "adequately capitalized."[11] This evasion came to light as part of a routine federal investigation into the failure of IndyMac.

IndyMac suffered a run on its US$19 billion in customer deposits in July as depositors withdrew more than US$1.3 billion from their accounts within 11 days of the release of Senator Schumer's letter. On July 9, the bank announced that it had been unable to raise new capital and would have to stop taking new loan applications and dismiss half of its 7,200 employees. On July 13, the

Federal Deposit Insurance Corporation (FDIC) took it into conservatorship in a rescue that cost an estimated US$4–US$8 billion. But the collapse of Bear Stearns, Countrywide, and IndyMac was just the beginning. The implosion was yet to come.

THE FALL OF FANNIE AND FREDDIE

Freddie Mac and Fannie Mae, the two government-supported enterprises operating in the mortgage market, were nationalized on September 8. Fannie and Freddie were subject to schizophrenic illogic of being both private enterprises maximizing profits and quasi-public enterprises with the mandate of increasing affordable mortgages for families. Both agencies buy mortgages from lending institutions and then either hold them in investment portfolios or resell them as MBSs to investors. Apart from selling MBSs, they also guarantee these securities and are obliged to buy back the mortgage in case of default. This guarantee which was implicitly perceived to be a government guarantee helped boost the supply of credit by enabling these agencies to buy huge amounts of mortgages from commercial banks. But with the increasing involvement of Wall Street investment banks in the mortgage business—including the subprime and Alt-A mortgages—the share of Fannie and Freddie in the market for MBSs began falling during the housing boom. In an attempt to reclaim the market and their revenues, Fannie and Freddie began in the recent years to buy MBSs from the Wall Street banks, including those based on subprime and Alt-A loans.[12]

The mortgage meltdown paradoxically heightened the importance of these two agencies. Fannie and Freddie began to reassert their central role in mortgage finance. As the subprime crisis unfolded in 2007, Fannie and Freddie stepped into the breach as private-label mortgages seized up. The ceiling on the maximum value of the mortgages they could purchase was raised. The reserve capital requirements were eased. The two agencies that in 2005 had a share of about 40 percent of the market for MBSs now saw their share rise to about 80 percent. This surge in market share was effected on a tiny sliver of capital. The two agencies had together borrowed to the extent of about 65 times their capital base. By July 2008, the losses due to write-downs in their asset base were about US$45 billion. From US$60 a share in 2007 their stock price sank below US$10 a share in July 2008—a fall of about 80 percent. The agencies were faced with the prospect that their creditors would balk at rolling over their short-term loans fatally endangering the already teetering mortgage market. With about 20 percent of the Fannie and Freddie debts being owned by foreign investors, the potential fallout was immense.[13]

On July 13, a Sunday Treasury Secretary Paulson stepped in to extend the lines of credit available to Fannie and Freddie, and allowed these agencies to borrow from the Fed's discount window, further widening the access to this window. The estimated cost of this rescue was US$25 billion to sustain US$5,200 billion of mortgage credits of which 15 percent were from riskier categories of lenders.

More portentous was the bald statement that the Treasury would, if necessary, exercise the option of a "temporary authority to purchase equity in either of the two [companies]." By making a traditionally implicit government guarantee for the mortgage debt increasingly explicit, the Treasury was basically pinning its hope on the fact that such a guarantee was enough to reassure foreign and domestic investors by providing a safety net. Paulson actually told the Senate banking committee: "If you've got a squirt gun in your pocket, you probably will have to take it out. If you have a bazooka in your pocket and people know it, you probably won't have to take it out." [14]

By the end of the month of July, these sanguine hopes were belied as investors essentially called the Treasury's bluff and showed a limited appetite for debt and preferred stock issued by Fannie and Freddie. The share prices continued to tumble. Asian investors, in particular, grew increasingly wary and started pulling out of the market for agency debt. Between June and August, Bank of China, China's fourth largest commercial bank, offloaded a quarter of its portfolio of securities issued or guaranteed by Fannie and Freddie (amounting to around US$4.6 billion). At the same time the attempts by Freddie and Fannie to seek capital from private investors did not land any takers.

On August 8, Paulson finally pulled out the bazooka placing the two agencies into conservatorship. The plan committed up to US$200 billion over the following year for recapitalizing the agencies through purchases of preferred stock and also committed the treasury to buying chunks of the agency MBSs (beginning with a US$5 billion purchase in September itself). The markets were still not convinced. Panic continued to spread like a contagion.

Bringing Lehman Down

On September 15, Lehman Brothers, an investment bank with a 158-year history filed for bankruptcy after making huge losses on the bets it had made on real estate. From its inception as a modest cotton-trading firm in Alabama started by two German immigrant brothers in 1850, the company moved to New York City after the Civil War and has since then traversed a fairly bumpy ride (including being taken over by American Express in 1984 before splitting off again in 1991) from a small bond-trading house into an influential player on Wall Street. It was the second of the haloed circle of the five major investment banks to crumble.[15]

Just the previous year in May 2007, Lehman had bought up Archstone-Smith Trust, a property investment company owning a giant portfolio of apartments in "the most desirable" neighborhoods of large US cities, in a deal amounting to about US$20 billion. The deal was sealed at the peak of the bubble. Richard Fuld, the CEO, had committed the cardinal Wall Street sin of buying at the top of the market. This deal proved to be a harbinger of the downfall of Lehman as Archstone became part of a crippling US$30 billion-plus in property assets that the bank would be unable to sell. Worth US$60 billion a few weeks before this ill-conceived deal, Lehman was worth only US$2 billion in the first week of September 2008.

But even before this, Lehman had been struggling for many months to shore up its balance sheet, securing a US$2 billion credit line from its banks on March 14—even as the Federal Reserve was brokering the JPMorgan Chase takeover of Bear Stearns. Fuld, a member of the board of governors of the New York Federal Reserve, is reputed to have been a major force behind the Federal Reserve's decision to allow investment banks to borrow from the discount window after the Bear Stearns fiasco. In fact after Bears Stearns was brought down, Lehman was widely perceived as the next target for speculators and the Federal Reserve measure was referred to as the "Save Lehman Act of 2008."[16] Access to the discount window was supposed to have preempted a

Bear-style run on the bank by assuring short-term credit. But there continued to be grave doubts about the actual value of Lehman's holdings—and Archstone assets in particular. Lehman reported a US$2.8 billion loss in June.

Despite the growing qualms Lehman cobbled together US$6 billion from other financial institutions. Lehman also began courting foreign capital. In the first week of August, Lehman held parallel talks with the government-owned Korea Development Bank and China's Citic Securities. While the talks with the Chinese never progressed very far, concrete arrangements were under discussion with the South Koreans. Under this procedure, the Korean bank would buy a 25 percent stake directly from Lehman and another 25 percent of the shares through a market tender. The price proposed by Lehman was 50 percent above Lehman's book value, and was finally deemed too high. Soon after the nationalization of Fannie and Freddie, the talks with the Korean lender stalled.

As the rumors permeated through the markets, events began spinning out control. The threat of credit downgrades sparked further sell offs and the stock plunged by 45 percent on September 10. In a desperate bid to quell the rumors, Lehman released its third-quarter results a week earlier than scheduled—placing on record a US$4 billion loss and laying out a drastic restructuring plan after its bid to secure capital from foreign investors failed. The plan involved selling most of its prized asset management unit, Neuberger Berman, selling US$4 billion in UK property assets to Blackrock and spinning off US$30 billion worth of troubled property assets into a separate entity—a kind of a "bad bank." This separate entity, after a capital injection of about US$7.5 billion, would hold the toxic assets to maturity, insulating the rest of Lehman, which would now reemerge as a smaller, less risky core. The free fall continued unabated. Shares, which sold for as much as US$67 in the past 12 months, began trading at US$3.65. The total losses since the mortgage markets seized up amounted to nearly US$15 billion.

By Thursday evening, September 11, Lehman was in full crisis mode, actively reaching out to a range of suitors. Paulson had made it quite clear that no government money would be forthcoming but had plunged into a flurry of deal brokering. What followed was a three-day scramble by top Wall Street executives and federal regulators to work out an acceptable solution. Ten years after the top Wall Street executives had been called upon to step up and help rescue LTCM, the hedge fund that collapsed in 1998, Paulson summoned Wall Street's top bankers, including Lloyd Blankfein of Goldman Sachs, John Mack of Morgan Stanley, and John Thain of Merrill Lynch, into an emergency meeting at the headquarters of the New York Fed to discuss a rescue of Lehman Brothers. The greatest hopes were pinned on Bank of America and Barclays. The bankers had been brought to the table to facilitate such a deal by shelling out funds to collectively purchase a "bad bank" containing Lehman's sequestered commercial real estate assets. The plan was a nonstarter as no Wall Street banker was willing to pay to acquire bad assets, only to make the way for a rival bank to acquire the famed investment bank. On Saturday, September 13, Bank of America walked away from the deal and instead turned its sights on acquiring Merrill Lynch. Later, the next day, Barclays too pulled out citing the intransigence of the US government on providing any sort of guarantees even temporarily to smoothen the takeover. In the meantime, Lehman's toxic assets had grown to nearly US$80 billion.

The fate of Lehman was sealed. It filed for bankruptcy on September 15. The next day Barclays said it would buy Lehman's US capital markets division for US$1.75 billion, while Nomura

Holdings of Japan claimed Lehman's European and Asian assets. Lehman's money management business, including Neuberger Berman, was sold to Bain Capital and Hellman & Friedman for US$2.15 billion. More than a year later, the bankrupt Lehman estate filed a lawsuit against Barclays Capital alleging that Barclays had structured the deal in connivance with Lehman executives in a manner that allowed it to pocket more than US$5 billion in windfall gains.

THE MERGER OF MERRILL LYNCH

The travails of Lehman had in the meantime prompted Merrill Lynch to court the Bank of America as a potential buyer. Founded in 1914, Merrill Lynch was the third of the five major investment banks on Wall Street, one that prided itself on being the main stockbroker for Main Street as well.

In October 2007, the firm that boasted a corporate logo that was a hard-charging bull, shocked investors when it announced a US$7.9 billion write-down related to its exposure to MBSs, resulting in a US$2.3 billion loss, the largest in the firm's history. In the ensuing shake-up, the longtime CEO, Stanley O'Neal, was replaced by John Thain who was entrusted with the task of staunching the flow of losses.

Even as the fate of Lehman was being discussed in the meeting on September 12, John Thain and Ken Lewis (CEO, Bank of America) were discussing the possibility of a merger. In what was in retrospect a "shot-gun marriage," Bank of America agreed after rapid discussions over the course of the weekend to pay US$50 billion in stock, offering US$29 per share for Merrill Lynch, after the stock had closed at US$17.05 on the preceding Friday. Both Bank of America and Merrill Lynch were in a rush to announce the broad contours of a deal before the markets opened on Monday, so decisions that would typically be the subject of painstaking advanced negotiations were left to be sorted out later.[17]

Bank of America had already bought up Countrywide Financial, diversifying its operations in the mortgage sector. The deal with Merrill Lynch offered the seductive prospect of combining its huge commercial lending operations with Merrill Lynch's prime retail brokerage and the "crown jewel" of Merrill's 17,000 financial advisers.

The real skills of these "crown jewels" became clear by December as magnitude of the losses on Merrill Lynch's books gradually emerged. Merrill Lynch hemorrhaged US$15.3 billion during the final three months of 2008 alone.[18] Bank of America's shareholders did not learn of the gaping hole in Merrill Lynch's books until after they approved the merger of the two companies on December 5. In fact the full magnitude of the losses was not revealed after Merrill had paid out US$3.6 billion in bonuses (based on estimates of the firm's performance as of December 8), moving up the bonus payments to December, just before the merger was to be closed! John Thain is supposed to have initially asked for a US$40 billion bonus as recognition for shepherding Merrill safely into the arms of the Bank of America and spent US$1.2 million for a lavish office renovation for his brief tenure as Merrill head. These disclosures put paid to the plans of Thain taking over from Lewis in the new merged global "supermarket" bank that would be established after the merger.

As the details of the mess at Merrill were revealed, Ken Lewis initially balked at going through with the marriage and on December 17, he told Mr Paulson and Mr Bernanke that he was planning to invoke a "material adverse change" clause in the merger agreement that would have allowed the bank to walk away from the transaction. Paulson issued a strong signal against any such a move that might create a systemic risk to the financial system. It is rumored that the threat of removal and the dismantling of the company's board if Lewis failed to follow through with the deal were held out. What Lewis did manage to get in return for being "pressured" by regulators to complete the deal was a second emergency infusion of US$20 billion in capital (in addition to the US$25 billion it had received earlier as part of the Treasury rescue efforts). In fact, in April 2009, as the deal continued to draw heavy criticism, shareholders voted to strip Lewis of his title as chairman.

Since then there have been SEC allegations that Bank of America made false and misleading statements to shareholders about bonuses promised to Merrill employees. The Bank of America reached a settlement on August 3, 2009, to pay US$33 million to settle claims, without admitting or denying the accusations that it had misled its shareholders about the bonuses. This settlement was rejected by the New York district court as being too low and the Bank has subsequently been trying to reach a settlement for the sum of US$150 million. All this, however, was in the future. In the present, the crisis was continuing to fell giants. Next in line was the giant insurer American International Group (AIG).

SAVING THE INSURER

AIG with its origins as an agency providing insurance in Shanghai in 1919 grew to become a huge transnational insurance group, which was by the turn of the century the dominant provider of commercial and industrial insurance, one of the biggest writers of life insurance and the biggest provider of fixed (retirement) annuities in the United States. In the 1980s, the company was persuaded of the potential profits that could be reaped by spreading out from its staid role in insuring traditional risks (like death, accidents, and fires) to embark on the uncharted territory of insuring risks in rapidly evolving financial markets. The AIG Financial Products (AIGFP) arm was set up with a core group from former employees of Drexel Burnham Lambert, the company that had with its aggressive promotion of junk bonds been at the heart of the savings and loans crisis of the 1980s. The Financial Products arm became a way of hitching onto the bandwagon of the booming business of financial innovations earning huge fees and profits for the firm, while piling on greater and greater risks instead of insuring against them. This business of deploying AIG's low funding costs to create products that provided insurance against a range of financial risks (including the risk of default) bloomed under Maurice Greenberg, the head of company. Since 1998, AIGFP expanded its services to insuring investors against defaults on the opaque and exotic new instruments that Wall Street was engineering. By 2003, AIG was insuring portions of subprime mortgage deals and held a vast pile of securities linked to mortgage bonds.[19]

Goldman Sachs in particular had structured a group of deals— known as Abacus—which was actually packages of AIG insurance written against mortgage bonds. The deals would allow Goldman to make huge profits from a housing collapse and AIG was obligated to make large payments if the housing market ran aground. Goldman Sachs also used financing from other banks like Société Générale to purchase less risky mortgage securities from competitors and then insure the assets with AIG. By the late 2006, the firm had begun to make huge trades that would pay off if the mortgage market soured even as it continued to push the sales of these risky assets to its clients. The more mortgage securities prices fell, the greater were Goldman's potential profits.[20]

When the mortgage markets started unraveling in the summer of 2007, AIGFP executives professed a sanguine lack of unconcern, presenting estimates that assured investors that in the worst-case scenario it ran the risk of losing US$2.4 billion on the portfolio.[21] Through the summer, as the mortgage markets unraveled, Goldman Sachs called in its bets (and also pressed Société Générale to do the same) and AIG had paid out US$2 billion to Goldman Sachs by November 2007. The dispute began to escalate as AIG claimed that Goldman's valuation of the underlying assets had overestimated the damages inflating potential losses and demanded a return of a portion of what it had paid out, while Goldman Sachs countered that it was actually owed even more money while refusing to allow a third-party consultant to assess the value of underlying securities. Goldman proved to be tough negotiators and between July 2007 and August 2008 Goldman collected more than US$7 billion from AIG. The irony is that without the insurer to provide credit insurance, Goldman Sachs (which did not own the underlying bonds but had sold them and then bet against them) could not have generated the profits it made by betting against the mortgage market, but the implosion of the mortgage market would end up decimating AIG.[22]

By the third quarter of 2008, AIG's losses had reached US$25 billion. The company had burned through its equity. Once the biggest insurance company in the world, its market capitalization fell to just over US$7.5 billion. The collapse of Lehman was the last straw. As the shock wave spread through financial markets, AIG debt was downgraded, compelling AIG to come up with billions of dollars immediately to pay banks whose securities it had insured even as its share value plummeted. The potential fallout of the bankruptcy of a major insurance behemoth right after the

Lehman debacle was frightening. If AIG failed, a host of institutions that thought they were insured against default would suddenly find themselves exposed.

Yet another emergency meeting was called, hosted by the New York Federal Reserve with JPMorgan Chase, representing AIG, and Goldman Sachs, representing potential principal investors, in a bid to come up with some kind of funding facility to facilitate AIG tide over the crisis. Tim Geithner, then president of the New York Fed, even skipped the Fed's interest-setting meeting to focus on the AIG situation. Any plan to try to raise some US$70 billion in loans from investors had been derailed by the credit downgrades and the sharp fall in AIG's shares. The bankers argued that there was no alternative to a government rescue. While it was necessary to carve out and separate AIG's profitable traditional insurance operations from the troubled portfolios of credit insurance, the degree of interconnectedness between divisions and departments made the task quite a formidable one.

During a frantic day of emergency meetings at the New York Fed, the Treasury and Fed swallowed its reluctance to bail out another financial institution. A day after Lehman's bankruptcy filing, the Fed stepped in with a US$85 billion loan to rescue AIG on September 16. The amount of funds channeled to AIG would amount to US$182 billion over the next year. This bailout would be later subject to severe contention and scrutiny not least on the bonuses paid to the executives within the group.

FROM MELTDOWN TO A FREEZE

With the events of the second week of September 2008, the bursting of the bubble in one corner of the financial markets metastasized into a systemic crisis. The collapse of Lehman, followed within 24 hours by the rescue of AIG, was the turning point.[23] Overnight faith in the financial system evaporated and credit froze. Banks stopped lending to each other. Investors were so spooked that they began buying insurance (against defaults) at more than 30 times what they would normally pay. Even money market mutual funds which have generally been perceived to be as safe as deposit accounts (a safe place to store cash and earn interest on that money), and had held as much as US$3.4 trillion, were suddenly besieged by people wanting to pull out money after the Money Market Mutual Fund—Reserve Primary Fund that held a chunk of Lehman liabilities—"broke the buck" and began to make a loss. Soon firms and businesses found their short-term funding squeezed as the commercial paper market froze. The only safe asset in the meltdown was the debt of the US state—US treasury bills. The interest rates on US treasury bills dropped to near zero as investors flocked to buy US treasury bills.

The financial system was gripped by a complete breakdown of credit. The magnitude of the crisis evoked the specter of the Great Depression. The foundations of the financial system seemed to be on the brink of collapse. On Thursday, September 18, in a hastily convened meeting on Capitol Hill, with congressional leaders to urge a swift "break the glass" rescue of the financial markets, Bernanke is said to have pleaded: "If we don't do this, we may not have an economy on Monday." It was in the words of Alan Greenspan, "a once in a century credit tsunami." Except that it was completely man-made.

How could the collapse of the housing bubble and rising defaults in the riskier fringes of the mortgage market bring the entire credit machinery grinding to a halt? The answer lies in the manner in which banking and finance had evolved in the past decades.

Chapter 3

The House of Cards

When the music stops, in terms of liquidity, things will be complicated.
But as long as the music is playing, you've got to get up and dance. We're
still dancing.

—Charles Prince, CEO Citigroup, *Financial Times*, August 9, 2007

In the panic that engulfed the financial system after the collapse
of Lehman and the takeover of Merrill Lynch, the two US investment banks that remained standing—Goldman Sachs and Morgan
Stanley—also felt the brunt of the shock waves from the imploding markets. They had continued to make profits through the collapse of the subprime markets but their shares now went into a
freefall. Their balance sheets began hemorrhaging, and both were
forced to seek infusions of capital—Morgan Stanley from Mit-
subishi UFJ Financial Group (in a deal worth up to US$9 billion
for a 20 percent stake) and Goldman Sachs from Warren Buffett
(an injection of US$5 billion in the form of preference shares) to
shore up their balance sheets. As the markets continued to unravel,
John Mack (CEO, Morgan Stanley) and Lloyd Blankfein (CEO,
Goldman Sachs) took the dramatic decision to take their banks
into the supervisory arms of the Federal Reserve. This would give
them easier access to liquidity support and a more diverse funding
base, including retail deposits. On September 22, the last two remaining US investment banks were transformed into bank holding

companies. It seemed, for a while, as if the era of the Wall Street investment bank had come to a close.

THE RISE OF THE BROKER-DEALER

The pure investment bank was, in a sense, the creation of the Glass-Steagall Act of 1933 that enforced the separation of investment and commercial banking. This act was a response to the catastrophic experience of the Great Depression. This separation between the two functions has been gradually eroded since the 1980s. During the 1980s, the US financial system was rocked by the savings and loans crisis in which a slew of thrift institutions got wiped out. In the wake of the crisis, restrictions on commercial banks from affiliating with firms "engaged principally" in underwriting and dealing in securities were relaxed, as were the restrictions on broker-dealer firms and insurance companies to acquire certain types of depository and thrift institutions. The Gramm–Leach–Bliley Act, 1999 (also known as the Financial Services Modernization Act, FSMA) finally gave legislative sanction to the blurring of lines between security traders and deposit bankers, and repealed key provisions of the Glass–Steagall Act. Holding company owners of commercial banks were now allowed to engage in all types of financial activity and to own subsidiaries engaged in a broad range of financial activities. Citibank (a commercial bank holding company), for instance, had merged with Travelers Insurance Group and Solomon Smith Barney to evolve into a financial conglomerate Citigroup that combined banking, securities, and insurance services. The passage of the FSMA gave this merger legal sanction. J.P. Morgan and Chase Manhattan merged in 2000 to form JPMorgan Chase, and later swallowed Bank One.

In fact by 2008, the firms regarded as investment banks had already become large financial conglomerates. With the metamorphosis of Goldman Sachs and Morgan Stanley into holding companies, this evolution has come full circle. The pure investment bank model—where the prime broker-dealer engaged in underwriting, issuing, and trading securities on behalf of clients including corporations or government and was outside the ambit of the safety net that the Federal Reserve provided deposit banks—was in a sense institutionalized in response to the crisis of the Great Depression. The last remnants of this model which sought to set up a firewall between commercial and investment banking has been finally brought down in the wake of the current crisis.[1] The financial terrain had, however, already been significantly transformed over the previous three decades.

Traditionally, the revenues of investment banks were generated from commissions on trade on behalf of clients. With the abolition of fixed fee commissions in 1975, banks found this source of its earnings increasingly limited, and began a scramble to search for more innovative ways of boosting earnings. Instead of standard plain vanilla contracts that traded in the exchanges and garnered fixed commissions, the bankers in a quest for new sources of earnings began to push toward crafting customized instruments for individual clients in over-the-counter transactions with individually negotiated fees.

Salomon Brothers (which was later incorporated into Citigroup) had pioneered the idea of having a proprietary trading desk betting its own capital on movements in markets at the same time as the bank bought and sold securities on behalf of its customers.[2] This practice became widespread and investment banks began to increasingly trade on their own account (what is called proprietary trading) rather than focusing primarily on trading on behalf of their clients. The principal business of advising clients on corporate finance and investment matters became subsumed in a dash for profit involving principal investing and proprietary trading. In the process, the lines between what the banks were doing for themselves and what they were doing for clients were blurred.[3]

One of the innovations of the period was the mortgage-backed security (MBS). The bank purchased a mortgage loan from a mortgage company. It then issued a new tradable asset—the MBS—that represented claims on the cash flows—principal and interest payments—generated by mortgage loans. The basic conception of the MBS has been widened since the 1980s to forge a securitization machine that generates huge fee and commission income by cranking out novel financial products. The practice spread to the issue of asset-backed security (ABS) against a broader class of loans—for example, auto loans. The low interest regime of the 1990s spurred further innovations in financial engineering as a way to generate profits, enabling a massive expansion of Wall Street trading activities.

The assets of US investment banks have grown from about 3 percent of US gross national income in 1975 to about 24 percent of gross domestic product (GDP) in 2007. In the same period the assets of Bank Holding Companies grew from 4 to 16 percent of gross national product (Figure 3.1). The combined balance sheets of the five major investment banks grew to total US$4 trillion in 2007, while the total assets of the top five bank holding companies in the US at that point were just over US$6 trillion.[4]

The funding for this vastly expanded scale of operations was drawn increasingly from money market funds, mutual funds, and pensions funds. A major source of borrowing was the short-term market—commercial paper and the repo market. Commercial paper is a promissory note, usually with a maturity of less than 180

Figure 3.1. The Growth of the Broker-Dealer (Investment Banks and Bank Holding Companies as a Share of Gross National Income)

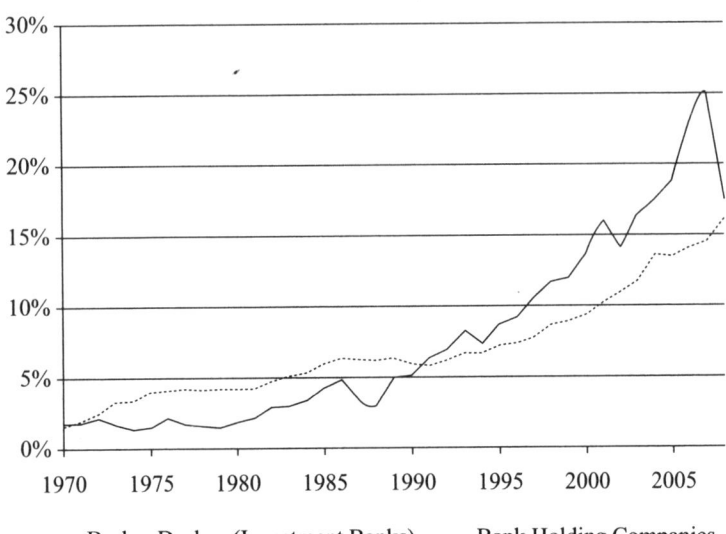

——— Broker Dealers (Investment Banks)　········Bank Holding Companies

Source: Federal Reserve: Flow of Funds.

days, which is issued by major banks (and also corporations) to meet short-term debt obligations. The commercial paper of reputed institutions with a high credit standing can be backed solely by the borrowers "promise to pay." Commercial paper can also be issued against the collateral of physical or financial assets (called asset-backed commercial paper).

The repo is a repurchase agreement where the bank posts a security as collateral for a loan with the promise that it will buy the security back when the loan is repaid. This market allowed the investment bank to buy an asset by borrowing money using this same asset as collateral. The bank repays this loan through the proceeds of the sale of the security (which is still being held as collateral with the lender) and on repayment of the loan "buys

38

back" the security, which is promptly passed on to the purchaser. Hefty profits are churned out as long as asset prices are rising.

The investment banks in their frenzy for returns took on greater and greater debt in order to finance their growing asset base. Borrowing was pushed to the limit, since this debt could be reinvested into highly profitable trades that earned higher returns than the cost of borrowing–chasing "leverage" in the jargon. Typically, leverage is measured as the ratio of equity to assets or the equity to debt.[5] A higher leverage implies a smaller equity base is deployed to acquire a given volume of assets. Targeting a leverage ratio pushes banks to take on more debt when asset prices increase during a boom. As the value of equity rises, the debt to equity ratio falls and the bank seeking to target its leverage would then take on more debt to acquire more assets while maintaining this leverage. While enabling a huge expansion in assets and returns when the going was good, this strategy that pushed banks to take on more and more debt left the banks vulnerable when asset prices collapsed and leverage shot up. The process of expanding debt and the balance sheet would now get reversed and banks would have to sell off assets to maintain their asset equity ratio.[6] In practice, leverage levels rose considerably through the period.

The financial landscape that emerged in the 1990s was thus one in which capital markets (where securities are traded) emerged as a significant site mediating borrowing and lending activity. Instead of depending on deposits, the financial intermediaries borrow by issuing short-term commercial paper or through repos. Lending activity is channeled through the sale of a variety of financial assets rather than loans. The investment banks underwrote and sold increasingly complex instruments to hedge funds and private equities with a high appetite for risk. Quite often the buyer could be another investment bank or their affiliates or subsidiaries. Financial markets were also becoming more globally integrated as deregulation and the lifting of capital controls began to open up lucrative offshore markets to US banks, serving as further fodder to this dizzying growth of finance. At the heart of the massive expansion of credit and financial flows was the process of "securitization"— the boom in the volume of securities traded.

Assets in the security issuing and trading sector grew to more than 450 times their 1970 magnitude by 2007 (Figure 3.2). This growth outpaces the growth of the other major sectors including commercial banking, which grew to 20 times its 1970 magnitude and nonfinancial firms that grew fortyfold in the same period. In 1980, about 27 percent of private nonfinancial sector debt was channeled through the security markets. By 2007 this share had grown to more than half.[7] This unbridled expansion of securitization was

Figure 3.2. The Securities Boom (Assets: 1970 = 1)

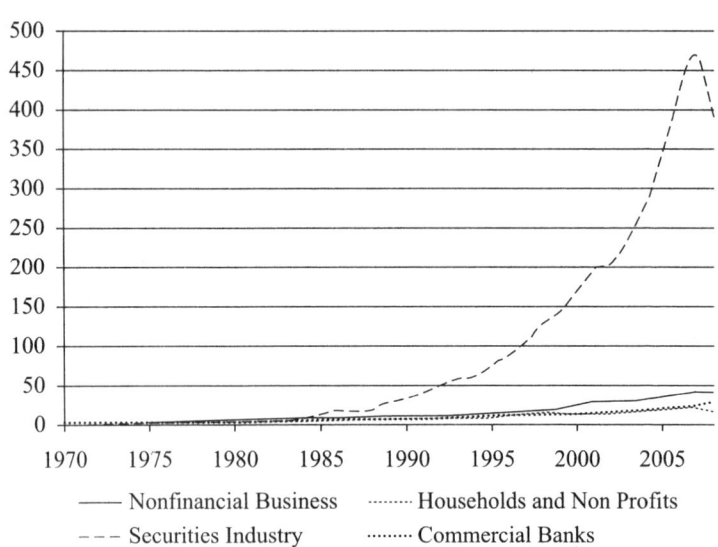

—— Nonfinancial Business ········ Households and Non Profits
– – – Securities Industry ········ Commercial Banks

Source: Federal Reserve: Flow of Funds.

40

central to the dizzying rise of the financial sector, and to the specific form in which the credit crunch seized the markets.

THE ALCHEMY OF FINANCE

Securitization transforms future streams of income (from profits, dividends, or interest payments) into a tradable asset like a stock or a bond. The future earnings of corporations are transmuted into equity stocks that are bought and sold in the capital market. Likewise, a loan or a mortgage that involves certain fixed interest payments over its duration gets a new life when it is converted into marketable bonds (like the MBS and ABS). The next leap is to take pools of such assets, chop and bundle them together, repackage these into novel kinds of instruments, and then sell them in capital markets. This broad class of instruments is called collateralized debt obligation (CDO). Figure 3.3 illustrates the steps in this process.

Strictly speaking, the CDO is created as a separately managed fund that has bought the ABS from a mortgage originator (Figure 3.3). To do so, the CDO then slices and dices this pool and then sells tranches (equity, mezzanine, and senior) of this mishmash to other investors. The buyers of these bonds are paid off in a specific order depending on the tranche they bought into. The tranches represent different levels of risk and returns. All tranches draw from the same pool of loans but the safest senior tranche, which also yields a smaller return, has first claim on the cash flows from the pool. The chances of default on these securities are deemed extremely slim. The riskiest junior or equity tranche on the other hand was positioned to take the first hit when defaults occurred but also offered higher returns. The whole bundle could in the end be sold for more than the value of underlying assets.[8]

41

Figure 3.3. Securitization

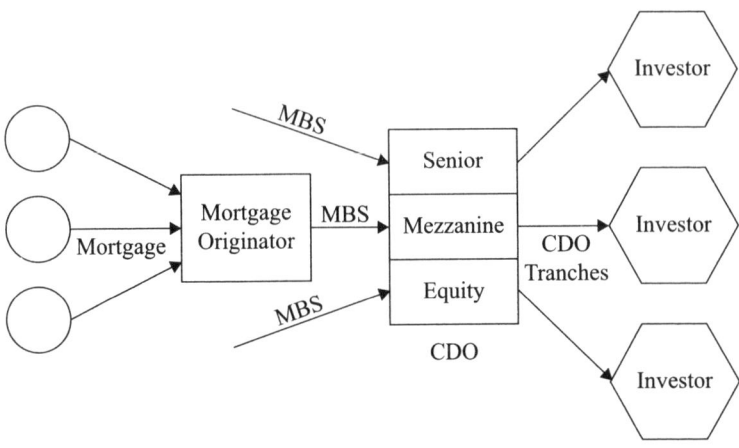

Source: Author's own.

Note: Mortgages are originated by a mortgage bank which then issues MBS against these loans. The MBS is bought by a bank to create a CDO. The pool of mortgages then gets sliced into different tranches and is sold to the investors.

The profitable business of securitization generated an alphabet soup of esoteric financial products that claimed to manage risk by dispersing it across investors. At the same time, it transmuted illiquid assets into a liquid source of funding. The schemes proliferated. CDOs were sliced and diced to create what were called CDO squared. And CDO cubed. As these instruments became more complex and opaque, it became increasingly impossible to assess exactly what kind of risk was the investor taking on when buying a slice of a pool of loans. The investor could no longer look at the credit history of the specific borrower when assessing the risk of default.

Instead, the idea was investors would actually choose the level of risk they wanted and the services of "independent" credit rating agencies such as Standard & Poors, Moody, or Fitch were called in to bless these exotic instruments with their stamp. These agencies were the high priests of the financial markets. If they rated a security AAA, it was deemed virtually riskless while lower ratings signified greater riskiness. Investors relied on these ratings for guidance in the maze of arcane finance. The models used by these agencies to assess risk were made available to the banks so that even before the securities were officially rated, the banks could gauge what the rating was likely to be and fine-tune the "engineering" to the desired rating. The small group of large banks that engineered these financial products wielded considerable clout over the rating agencies. The agencies could lose the huge fees they garnered if they gave unfavorable ratings and faced the perverse incentive to whitewash the potential risks. Since the 1970s these service fees had become the principle source of revenues of these agencies, creating an obvious conflict of interest. Since the fees from rating complex securities was much higher than that of rating plain vanilla products, these agencies were happy to overlook the inherent risks and provide high ratings to the structured securities.

The next step for the bank was to insure against the risk of default. In 1993 when Exxon was faced with a host of claims after the disastrous oil spill from its tanker Valdez, it took out a US$4.8 billion credit line from J.P. Morgan. J.P. Morgan came up with the novel idea of transferring the risk of an Exxon default to the European Bank for Reconstruction and Development (EBRD) without transferring the actual loan in what came to be called a credit default swap (part of the class of credit derivative contracts).[9] In return for annual fees EBRD would assume the risk of a default on the Exxon loan. Credit default swaps became a roaring business—offering a way for investors to take bets on the outcomes of loans, mortgages, or bonds that they did not own. These insurance contracts would pay off in the event of a default or failure, but the buyer did not need to own the investment in order to collect.

The banks next came up with the idea of selling bundles of such credit derivatives contracts that insured a third party against the risk of default. The credit default swaps on a variety of loans (mortgages, for instance) taken out from investors were sliced and diced and resold. This was the synthetic CDO. The securitization idea was being stretched in unprecedented ways. Unlike the Exxon swap, where the contract was based on a specific contract with a specific debtor, the synthetic CDO represents a slice of the risk of a pool of credit default swaps. The investor underwriting the insurance of the new financial product could ignore the details about the riskiness of individual assets underlying the synthetic CDO because the engineering offered a deceptively easy way of calibrating risk.

These instruments marked a sea change in the manner in which risk was managed. Banks could underwrite the securitization of loans of their client, sell these to investors and at the same time buy a credit default swap that insured against the risk the deal would go sour. The beauty of this scheme was that the bank did not need to take on any of the risk of the original loan. The alchemy of finance, it seemed, had banished risk, transmuting it into a lucrative source of fees and commissions. It was no longer a simple way of hedging against risk, but a device for huge speculative gains for the buyer of the swap. Companies like AIG got into this game, writing swaps that provided it with regular payments in exchange for taking on a third party's risk of default. Spurred by the immense possibilities opened up by this form of insurance, banks began to keep on its books some of the tranches of the CDOs they were churning out. From a value of about US$70 billion in

2000, CDO transactions peaked at over US$500 billion in 2006, before falling to around US$480 billion in 2007. Synthetic CDOs accounted for about 10 percent of the total CDO sales.[10]

Banks had lurched into territory that by any sane definition was fraudulent, if not criminal. A case in point is the notorious Abacus deal (valued at about US$10.9 billion), brokered by a unit of Goldman Sachs at a point when the bank expected a downturn and had turned bearish on the state of the mortgage market. The deal comprised of synthetic CDOs created out of a pool of credit default swaps taken out against a chunk of mortgages. These underlying mortgage securities were handpicked in consultation with the Paulson Hedge funds. The deal was set up to fail. This vital information was not disclosed to its clients while the Goldman Sachs team aggressively marketed the Abacus CDOs. These clients included affiliates of ABN-AMRO and IKB, banks that took the first hit as the subprime market collapsed. Goldman Sachs (and the Paulson Fund) in the meanwhile bet that the CDO would default, pocketing rich returns (US$14 billion in profits in 2009) apart from the US$15 million in fees for brokering the deal![11] Phil Angelides who heads the Financial Inquiry Commission likened this to selling a used car with bad brakes and then buying insurance on the driver!

All the pieces were in place for a huge bonanza and the subsequent collapse. Investment banks took a pool of illiquid and risky assets and then sliced and diced them into a new-structured security. Once these were anointed by the credit rating agencies, they sold them to a range of buyers including mutual funds, pension funds, and hedge funds. The bank then turned around and bet against the security that it had been aggressively pushing to the investors by buying credit default swaps. These financial innovations were like conjuring tricks that allowed the investment banks to significantly reduce their capital reserves by using insurance bets to banish credit risk on their asset base and also find ways to simply move some of the riskier assets off their books.

IN THE SHADOW OF THE BANKING SYSTEM

The Basel standards that set an international benchmark for regulators constrain banks to maintain capital reserves equivalent to about 8 percent of the risk adjusted value of their assets. This limited the bank's ability to put its capital to work generating returns. Inventive means were found to move these deals off the bank's books and shift chunks of the securitization process to a network of off–balance sheet entities.

Holding companies and off–balance sheet affiliates were created to house the soaring assets of the banks and to carry out the slicing and dicing of loans. This came to be known as the "originate and distribute model."' Loans were taken out and then offloaded to these quasi-shell entities—Special Purpose Vehicles (SPVs), Special Investment Vehicles or Conduits—that would purchase these loans and repackage them into complex products. These entities were funded by borrowings from the short-term commercial paper market, including commercial paper backed by those same-structured financial products! By August 2007, about half of the US$2.2 trillion in commercial paper outstanding was asset backed.[12]

Since CDOs and other assets held by the shadow banks have longer maturities, there was a risk that when it came to the crunch, they would not have the funds to redeem this asset-backed commercial paper. In such an eventuality, it was the parent bank that would typically have to extend a credit line (for less than a year in order to evade Basel rules). This device allowed the banks to greatly reduce their capital reserves, freeing up capital to crank out more and more of these structured financial products.

Such shadow entities were at the center of Enron's operations in the 1990s, as it morphed from being an energy merchant to trading strange "commodities" such as weather futures and other energy derivatives. Even as its fortunes skyrocketed to make it one of US's largest companies, it developed a web of off–balance sheet vehicles and inscrutably opaque financial structures to hide its growing debts. Enron used these shell companies, with charming names like Raptor and JEDI, to funnel loans from banks. These loans were transformed into "trades" through swap transactions that Enron claimed were hedges for its commodities' trades. This sleight of hand allowed Enron to present its rising indebtedness as risk reduction. These manipulations were exposed after Enron's bankruptcy. While the banks—including Chase Manhattan (before merger) and Citibank—that had brokered these swaps were let off with a rap on the knuckles after reaching a settlement, Enron's auditors Arthur Anderson who had given their blessings to these dodgy bookkeeping were found criminally liable and eventually went out of business. Not surprising, then, that the lesson learnt was not to shun such dubious ploys and transactions but rather to continually strive to perfect the technique.

Many years later, Lehman used a similar derivative transaction—Repo 105—to make US$50 billion of debt vanish from its books. The conjuring trick involved Lehman using a US shadow vehicle to buy bonds from a bank, and then turning around and selling these bonds through an affiliate in London with the understanding that they would repurchased at 5 percent above the original sale price. A loan was disguised as a sale. Ernst and Young, one of the big four accounting companies (the other three being Price Waterhouse Coopers, Deloitte Touche Tohmatsu, and KPMG), had given its seal of approval to this accounting gimmick. Like the credit rating business, the business of auditing too was dominated by a few large concerns that were deeply beholden to their paymasters—the big banks.

The problem was not simply that of accounting fraud by Lehman, or Goldman's breach of trust in betting against its own clients. The problem was of the pervasive spread of the illusion that fancy financial engineering could banish risk, even as the securitization machinery allowed banks to increase liquidity much beyond the regulatory constraints imposed by monetary authorities. The securities that fueled this lucrative boom bore an extremely tenuous and opaque relation to the original loans and assets that they were derived from.

In the traditional system of banking, banks took in deposits and then lent out funds to investors based on evaluations of credit worthiness of each individual project. Deposits that can be withdrawn at will by the depositors are in a sense a short-term borrowing by the bank. The loans in contrast have a longer maturity. This is the essence of banking and credit creation—transforming short-term borrowings into long-term lending. This old system has given way to a new form of banking.[13] The off–balance sheet system that has developed in the shadow of the major banks acquires funds by issuing commercial paper, and instead of lending directly buys mortgage and ABS, slices, and dices them into new products that are then sold to other investors (Figure 3.4). It is the old business of banking—borrowing short and lending long—in a new form.[14] *At its peak, this shadow banking system held assets of approximately US$16 trillion, about US$4 trillion more than regulated deposit-taking banks.*[15] The difference is that it was being mediated through capital markets largely outside the ambit of federal regulation.

Figure 3.4. Shadow Banking: Borrowing Short, Lending Long

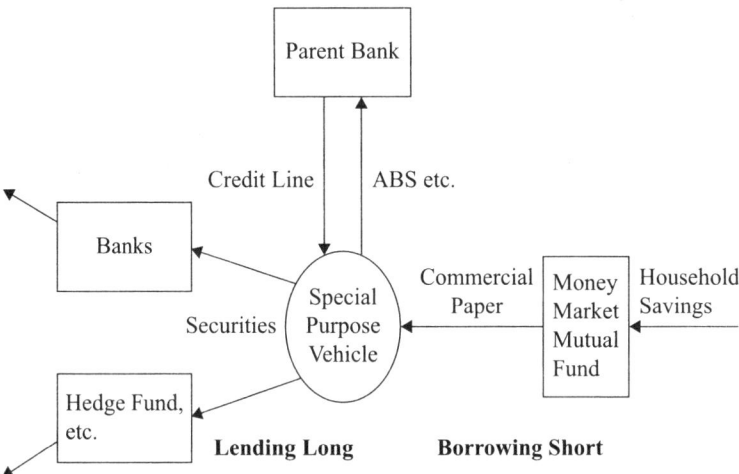

Source: Author's own.

Note: Savings are invested Money Market Mutual Funds which use these to buy commercial paper issued against the collateral of high-grade debt of SPVs (created by large parent banks). These SPVs are then deployed these short-term borrowings to buy ABS which were then transformed into new securities that were bought by investors, including hedge funds and banks.

Credit creation depends on the willingness of capital markets to buy commercial paper on the one end and securities on the other.[16]

The real magic of this seemingly endless flow of credit—the flood of liquidity that had been created—was the transformation of illiquid assets into liquid tradable instruments. Every financial asset has a risk of default associated with it. The safest and most liquid asset in the global financial market is the US Treasury Bill, which is backed by the guarantee of the US state. The returns on holding these treasury bills are, however, low. Securitization carved out what appeared to be a close substitute to the treasury bill from a pool of loans or other assets.[17] This high-grade debt did not enjoy a government guarantee but had been anointed by the ratings agencies, and could be traded and funded separately and was also perceived as suitable collateral for commercial paper in the money market.[18] In the era of low interest rates, pension funds and mutual funds (that mobilized private savings) were hard put to find assets that were liquid but offered a decent return. Any instrument that appeared safe but paid a higher interest rate than treasury bonds found ready buyers in this context. Money markets, the center of short-term lending, were drawn into funding this web of speculative trade.

At each stage in the web of transactions involved in slicing and dicing illiquid assets into tradable securities, the players involved from banks to ratings agencies to insurance companies, gained a big fee every time such a bond was issued. The investors driving this process took on massive amounts of debt (leveraging to about 30 times their asset base by 2007) and were much more highly leveraged than traditional banks. Their earnings depended on the premise that asset prices were unstoppable in their upward surge. Rising asset prices allowed them to take on more debt, churn out new products, and pocket rich earnings. As earnings across the industry rose, the stodgier bankers found themselves being pushed to the margins in the dizzy new world of shadow banking and financial engineering. This insatiable thirst for investment assets stoked the speculative manias of the dot-com boom and subsequently the housing bubble.[19]

HOOKED ON BUBBLES

The 1990s saw breakneck investment in new technology—the "new economy." Investment banks, hedge funds, and private equity groups thrived in those heady times of the "dot-com boom." In the wake of the WorldCom, Enron, and Global Crossings debacles, the euphoria fizzled out. Interest rates were slashed from 6.5 percent in December 2000 to 3.75 percent in the summer of 2001. After September 2001, these rates were dropped even further to around 1.75 percent. A quest for new avenues of earnings was sparked. The housing boom and the market for mortgage-related securities provided a fertile ground for the securitization business.

With pension funds, insurance companies, hedge funds, and other institutions displaying a new found appetite for new ways to invest their funds, Wall Street went full speed into the money spinning business of refashioning mortgages into more liquid instruments. While commercial banks and savings banks have traditionally been the biggest lenders to homebuyers, by 2006, Wall Street investment banks had grabbed a commanding share of nearly 60 percent of the mortgage financing market.[20] The forays of investment banks with their tools of financial engineering creating CDOs out of the MBS turned illiquid and risky mortgage assets into tradable and immensely desirable tradable bonds, setting off a boom in the housing and mortgage markets.

Spurred by this tremendous appetite for mortgage-related securities, new mortgage lenders that entered the field drifted away from the traditional "conforming" home loans to extend credit on increasingly lax terms. Subprime and Alt-A borrowers were actively solicited and lenders like Countrywide and New Century Financial pursued blatantly predatory practices in baiting prospective homebuyers. Subprime originations grew from just US$160 billion in 2001 to US$625 billion in 2006, from about 8.6 to 20 percent of the total market. The percentage of subprime mortgages securitized in this period increased from half to 80 percent.[21]

An arsenal of new "affordability products" was deployed to widen the net of debtors. These included adjustable rate mortgages that hooked low-income borrowers with low teaser rates before tightening the noose and no income–no job–no asset loans that were taken out without any form of documentation. In 2005, the median first-time buyer put down only 2 percent of the sales price, and 43 percent made no down payment at all.[22] Homeowners were encouraged to refinance their mortgages and to cash in on home equity in the boom market, sinking them deeper and deeper in debt. Home equity loans grew from US$1 billion in 1980 to US$1 trillion in 2006.[23] Homeowners cashed almost US$5 trillion from their housing assets between 2001 and 2007 in the form of sales or borrowings against homes.[24]

While the "affordable housing mandate" during the Clinton era might have set the stage, this reckless borrowing was given a big push under the Bush regime through the initiative to promote the "ownership society." As housing became more unaffordable and out of reach, "the muscle of the federal government" was brought to bear to promote homeownership—from tax incentives to new goals for low-income lending, including a sanctioning of the predatory innovations in mortgage finance.

These questionable loans became grist for the securitization mill. CDOs based on the subprime loans were riskier but also offered higher returns. The only constraint to this booming business was the ability of the market to absorb these bonds and in the dizzying days of soaring house prices it seemed as if the money would never stop flowing. The market for home loans was like a bonanza providing ready money to borrowers and high returns to investors. When a lender extends a loan to a homebuyer, the credit history of the specific borrower is scrutinized to assess the risk and credit worthiness. The pools of debt from which this brew of securities was created were, however, anonymous. Buyers had to rely on the assessments of the bankers selling these securities or rating agencies that were paid by the banks to assess the securities. This booming industry was built on extremely flimsy foundations.[25]

As long as housing prices were soaring, the mortgage brokers, bankers, insurers, pension funds, mutual funds, and the rating and auditing agencies raked in the returns. Between 1998 and 2006 house prices nearly doubled (Figure 3.5). In 2006, there was a rise in the defaults on home loans, bringing this bonanza to a sputtering halt. Foreclosures spiked in the third quarter of 2007 to double the number in 2006. By November 2007, nearly 15 percent of subprime loans were in default, and two-thirds of the foreclosures filed for the year ending June 30, 2007 involved subprime loans.[26] With the spread of foreclosures, defaults, and delinquencies, housing

Figure 3.5. The Housing Boom

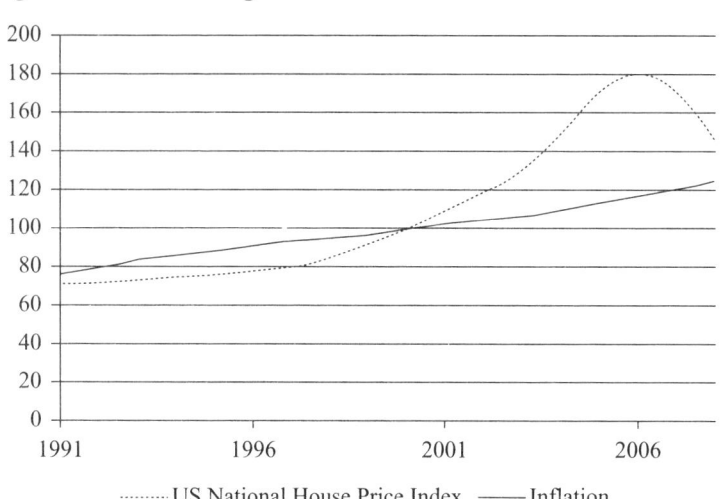

········ US National House Price Index ——— Inflation

Source: S&P Case/Shiller Index, US Bureau of Labor Statistics.

prices came tumbling down. Home buyers who were now in the hock for amounts much greater than the value of their homes were pushed to the brink. The spillover effects kept spreading. The crisis spread through the shadow banking system that had been built on the shaky edifice of these subprime loans.

PANIC

The unwinding of financial markets began with the collapse of the subprime mortgage market as the housing bubble lost steam. The increasing fears of default sent the rates on insurance (credit default swaps) on the complex securities and CDO's soaring, as investors began lapping up these swaps. This set off a collapse in the market for the underlying assets, spreading destruction. The pricing of the esoteric CDOs suddenly became fraught with uncertainty. The arcane models that sought to mimic open markets in the closed world of over-the-counter trades failed to comprehend the unfolding collapse. The shadow entities that had been churning out these structured products found themselves left with gaping holes in their asset base as the bottom fell out of the market for these securities. As the books of these banks became increasingly suspect, the market for the commercial paper issued against these assets too dried up.

A bank run conjures images of depositors queuing outside bank doors to pull out their funds. When panic gripped the markets after the Crash of 1929, leading to the Great Depression, the complete loss of faith in the banking system led to the frantic rush by depositors to pull their funds out of the banks as their confidence in the banking system was shattered. What was unfolding in 2008 was a very different kind of run—a run on the shadow banking system that had come to dominate credit creation. With investors refusing to roll over short-term debt, the spigot was turned off. This buyer's strike of commercial paper is the contemporary equivalent of the old-style bank run. The cumulative dynamic of the unfolding crisis transformed the liquidity problems into a larger one of bank insolvency.[27]

With shadow banks now forced to draw on the credit line of the parent bank, the big banks found the risk they thought they had banished from their books now steadily eating up their asset base. As these institutions began off-loading the now "toxic" assets in a process of deleveraging to restore their balance sheets, they set off a downward spiral in prices. The CDOs in the books of these banks were hot potatoes. With no one willing to touch these, prices hit rock bottom. Banks were forced to write down their assets in the face of these growing losses. The funding freeze that had afflicted the shadow banks engulfed the parent banks that had to find means of plugging this hole. Bear Stearns was the first US bank to fall, but all the major banks were exposed to this new form of a bank run. With the collapse of Lehman and the takeover of AIG in September 2008, the credit machinery seized up completely. Panicked investors thronged to assets that were considered safe and easily cashable.

This is the classic liquidity trap of Keynesian analysis. When investor confidence is brutally battered and uncertainty reigns, the preference for liquidity is absolute. So even if liquidity is pumped into the financial system, the banks remain averse to restarting lending and instead just stockpile the injections as reserves.

The economist Hyman Minsky,[28] while building on Keynes's key insights into the workings of the economy, had pointed to the endogenous generation of financial fragility within the capitalist financial structure—what has been dubbed the financial instability hypothesis. Periods of prosperity and high returns lull investors into taking on riskier positions and greater debt. As investors take on increasing amounts of debt to finance their positions, the financial system becomes more unstable, until lenders turn cautious and cut off the funds. This precipitates a systemic economic contraction.

Marx also had a remarkably prescient analysis of monetary crisis that foreshadowed the analysis of Keynes and Minsky. Marx had argued that capitalism's propensity to financial crisis arises "where the ever-lengthening chain of payments, and an artificial system of settling them, has been fully developed."[29] A credit crisis manifests the breakdown of "the chain of payments" that constitutes the financial system. This breakdown creates a frenzied clamor for "money" as the only safe asset as a "money famine" develops.[30]

The securitization industry had bred precisely such a chain of payments and settlements and the unraveling of the shadow banking system heralded a meltdown—what George Magnus, senior economic advisor at UBS, christened a "Minsky moment." What has unfolded is a classic debt deflationary spiral. The collapse of the credit mechanism to its monetary roots has been a classic sign of monetary crisis in the history of capitalism and the credit crunch of September 2008 is no different.

The bursting of the bubble unleashed investor panic. As the markets for these complex securities unraveled, banks and their shadow entities were confronted with huge write-downs in their asset base. This meant that the banks and their SPVs found it increasingly more difficult to roll over short-term debt as no one was willing to lend to the increasingly insolvent banks. This forced the banks to try to sell their assets at a time when the market for these assets had collapsed, further fueling the plunge in asset prices.

The "buyer's strike" of commercial paper turned off the spigot that had flooded the credit market with funds, and the evaporation of the market for securities exposed gaping holes in the balance sheets of financial institutions. What was unfolding was not simply a liquidity crunch that could be addressed by printing money, but more fundamentally the problem of the growing insolvency of financial institutions which were being forced to write-down their asset base. The ripple effects of the fall of Lehman and AIG threatened to take down the other financial institutions. The fragile foundations of the finance boom were exposed.

Keynes sought the euthanasia of rentiers and the sanitizing of these speculative propensities as the way to forestall this vulnerability to such recurrent crises. In the aftermath of the Great Depression, legislative and institutional changes were implemented to clip the wings of speculative finance and contain its impact on the larger economy. Marx went a step further to argue that the capitalist economic structure was entwined and rooted in this monetary financial system. It was the internal logic of this system that leads to the periodic outbreaks of crisis. Since this propensity was rooted in the economic structure, this tendency would continue to manifest itself. The capitalist economy may be a well-oiled machine, but it would sputter and jam with an alarming regularity.

The critical insights of Marx, Keynes, and Minsky into the pitfalls of the capitalist market economy have, however, been relegated to the dark corners of contemporary economic policy and theory. As even the more sanitized versions of Keynesian analysis were eclipsed by the rising neoliberal orthodoxy, policy consensus converged around an unwavering faith in the benign power of unfettered market forces. The celebration of the efficacy of markets has, in the past decades, come to encompass the workings of financial markets—the stomping ground of speculators and rentiers.

THE ECONOMIC PARADIGM

Finance serves a useful function in mediating flows of goods and services and in mobilizing and channeling savings into productive investments on a scale that would have been impossible without its intervention. The growth of finance, however, carries with it seeds of fragility as it breeds a tendency toward increasing speculation. Financial markets are a critical link in the outbreak and spread of panic and instability. The prices of financial assets reflect expectations of future earnings. They are consequently subject to wide swings in market sentiment, and investors make hefty returns by betting on such volatility—buying low and selling high.

This is, of course, a gamble, but unlike the toss of a coin, where the outcomes are known and can be assigned an equal chance of occurring, the future trajectory of asset prices is uncertain and unknown. Even more confounding, the actions of the investors can shape the course of these outcomes. This two-way feedback loop where the state of the market impinges on investor expectations and investor expectations affects the state of the market leads to the disruptive dynamics of boom–bust cycles. A euphoric rush to what is believed to be a market promising big returns generates a boom. Rising asset prices, for instance, in the housing markets lead to a flurry of buyers, stoking an already overheating market. The bust occurs when the prospects sour, and there is a stampede to exit the market.

In "the efficient markets" world of modern finance, these expectations are, however, supposed to accurately reflect the knowledge available to rational agents. Since prices adjust rapidly to new information and in effect move randomly, no speculator can beat the system for long. Despite this theorization, all the innovations in financial engineering did in fact attempt to beat the system—decomposing different elements of risks and finding ways to hedge against these. The complex pricing models developed by the financial industry, however, were built on a number of faulty premises that led to the systematic undervaluation of risk, while creating an illusion of providing greater protection.[31] These models in effect gave further license to the reckless pursuit of risk and leverage by fostering the complacent belief that risk could be dispersed, ignoring the possibility that a failure at a single point in this complex interconnected web of transactions could ricochet across the system to bring the pyramid of credit collapsing down. The pervasive neoliberal faith in the logic of the market further stoked the delusion of a never-ending bonanza.

The irony, of course, lay in the fact that in the arcane world of custom-built structured products and over-the-counter derivatives, the "models" spawned by the industry had usurped the role of the "market" of economic theory! As the conjurors of these models reaped fat profits from transactions that were conducted without any transparent process of price discovery through a market mechanism, they were immunized from the consequences of their actions. Bankers could recklessly bet huge sums of other people's money with an eye on short-term gains, pocket-hefty bonuses, and commissions, with no real liability if the deal later backfired. This created an agency problem typified in the "I'll be gone—You'll be gone" mind-set. The wizards of finance had an asymmetric command over the information, and sometimes actively disclosed only incomplete information to those who entrusted their money with them. The incentives of these bank executives were not aligned with that of their clients—the field was a hotbed of moral hazard and conflict of interest. These bankers with their models were in

essence playing a "market" game, without any fear of being pe-
nalized for their mistakes.

This absence of "material interest" in the form of market discipline was, paradoxically enough, part of the argument against the
socialist-planning project, during a debate that took place before
the Second World War between the advocates of capitalist markets
and the defenders of planning—the "socialist calculation debate."
Ludwig von Mises, an economist and philosopher of the Austrian
school, had argued that, even if planners sought to mimic price
signals, they could not create a disciplining mechanism analogous
to the market, and could not therefore capture capitalism's dynamism.[32] It would seem that neoliberal orthodoxy and the hegemony of market fundamentalism has been instrumental in bringing
into being a system plagued by this very failing!

The interconnected nature of the financial markets also creates
large externalities.[33] A failure at one link in the chain of payments
could quickly spiral into a string of defaults and bankruptcies. The
innovations that sought to disperse risk added to the complexity
and vulnerability of the web of transactions. These domino effects
mean that the actions of a few large and interconnected banks can
hold the society to ransom. This is the reason why, when the system implodes, the state has to step in. It is not simply that a few
banks are too big to fail, but that the costs of failure spiral out
through the economy and society in the form of lost jobs, fore-
closed homes, and bankruptcies.

The proximate cause of the crisis was undoubtedly the collapse
of the housing bubble. This bubble was fanned by the skewed
structure of incentives in the booming financial sector that had
got addicted to the money-spinning securitization euphoria. At
stake in the unraveling, however, is the neoliberal economic paradigm that provided the intellectual and ideological fodder to this

monstrous growth in finance. The scale of the crisis, its systemic roots, and impact make this a critical juncture to reexamine both the limitations of market and the current state of theorization of the functioning of these markets. In fact the crisis did spark some debate and introspection within the economics discipline.[34] Paradigms, however, are deeply embedded in institutions, and change slowly.

The immediate imperative in the wake of the crisis was that of preventing the spread of contagion from an imploding financial system from precipitating another Great Depression. The market, when it came to the crunch, needed to be rescued from the consequences of its own unbridled logic. The floundering and vacillation that was displayed on the policy front, stemmed in large part from the deep and pervasive hold of neoliberal ideology. The power and influence of Wall Street continued to shape the response of the US state even after its actions brought the economy to the brink.

Chapter 4

When Wall Street Rules
Main Street

And what I'm saying to you is, yes, I found a flaw ... a flaw in the model
that I perceived is the critical functioning structure that defines how the
world works, so to speak ... I made a mistake in presuming that the self
interest of organizations, specifically of banks and others were such that
they were best capable of protecting their own shareholders and their equity in firms.

— Alan Greenspan in testimony before House of Representatives
Committee on Oversight & Government Reform

The credit machinery that underlies the shadow banking system
thrived on the dizzying innovations in financial engineering. A
permissive policy regime that celebrated the ability of markets to
discipline and regulate itself helped nurture a culture of excessive
risk taking and leverage. The credit machinery was transformed
from the traditional deposit-based banking system to one based on
capital markets and securitization. Liquidity was created by transforming loans (in particular, mortgages) into marketable securities
and this thriving business was financed by borrowing using these
instruments as collateral to issue asset-backed commercial paper
and in repurchase agreements. What sparked the crisis was a new
form of a bank run, in the sense that the targets of panic have not
been bank deposits but the securities that have replaced them as

the prime generators of credit in the financial system. When the market for these securities dried up with the bursting of the housing bubble, credit creation was brought to a standstill.

A lot of the focus has centered on these financial instruments, whose toxicity is seen as the root of the financial crisis. The immediate policy imperative was to restart the broken credit apparatus and restore order to the discredited regulatory framework of the financial markets.

CLUTCHING AT STRAWS

Initial responses, still steeped in the unwavering faith in the inherent efficiency of financial markets and the monetarist belief that pumping liquidity into the financial system would stem the collapse, focused on attempts to restore confidence in the toxic assets and boost liquidity by lowering the interest rate and printing money.

In pursuing this course, Ben Bernanke was simply living up to his moniker, "Helicopter Ben." While the US was confronting the recessionary aftermath of the dot-com bust, he had argued that "if we fall into deflation, we can take comfort that the logic of the printing press will assert itself, and sufficient injections of money (what is called base money) will ultimately always reverse a deflation."[1] A scholar of the Great Depression, Bernanke, was deeply influenced by the economist, Milton Friedman, and believed that the Great Depression was prolonged by a failure to expand money supply. The appropriate strategy for arresting the downward spiral of asset prices is to foment inflation. A deflationary crisis like the Great Depression, in this worldview, could be dealt with simply by scattering freshly printed notes.

And so, one plank of the initial policy response was to expand the monetary base significantly. These injections were supposed to catalyze credit creation. The problem, however, was that these injections of "base money" did not translate into credit creation and an increase in money supply. Apart from such injections of base money, the Federal Reserve normally regulates the volume of credit in the economy by calibrating the Federal Funds rate (the rate at which banks lend surplus funds to one another) to expand or contract credit flows. The Federal Funds rate was brought down to 0.25 percent. The slashing of interest rates, however, had virtually no impact on kick-starting lending.

The breakdown in the financial system had prompted investors and banks to seek the safety of monetary assets and the bloated financial system collapsed to its fundamental monetary roots. There was a surge in demand for the low-yielding US Treasury Bill, which is indistinguishable from money in a context where money is the debt of the state. The injection of liquidity was not enough to revive credit flows since what was being witnessed was an insatiable demand for money—instead of spending or investment, money was being hoarded.

The Federal Reserve is responsible for regulating the flow of credit in the financial system. The financial system has, however, evolved much beyond commercial deposit banking and the process of repackaging loans into tradable instruments has enabled the shadow banking system to grow beyond the regulatory constraints of the Federal Reserve. Though the Federal Reserve had, by 1999, grown to be an "umbrella supervisor" of the entire range of US financial holding companies,[2] this evolution has greatly undermined the efficacy of traditional policy tools. Part of the US Federal Reserve's response to the implosion of the financial system has been an attempt to come to terms with this new financial landscape.

Rescuing the Banks

The revelations of the vulnerability of the largest banks posed a threat to the wider economy. The urgent need was to find means of injecting funds into these banks and plugging the holes in their balance sheets. The first initiatives were geared toward reviving the market for these assets by creating facilities to buy the toxic assets. As the markets began unwinding, the hope was that the large banks could be steered into solving their problem without public funds.

Citibank, which was particularly vulnerable because of its shadow vehicles, pushed for action under the aegis of the US Treasury and a proposal was mooted to set up a collectively funded SPV that would buy these beleaguered assets. Stewarded by the US Treasury, several major banks announced the setting up of a Super SIV (structured investment vehicle)—the Master Liquidity Enhancement Conduit (MLEC)—that would take on billions of dollars worth of toxic assets off the balance sheets of banks and their SIVs. This fund was, in a way, reminiscent of the fund that J.P. Morgan had engineered a century ago during the panic of 1907. By December, this superfund was abandoned as no bank was willing to finance what appeared to be the rescue of Citibank.

As collective solutions within the private-banking sector proved a failure, individual banks turned to sovereign wealth funds—state-owned investment funds held by countries with surplus reserves. Abu Dhabi Investment Authority and Singapore Investment Group invested in Citibank, China Investment Corporation in Morgan Stanley, Temasek, and Korean Investment Corporation in Merrill Lynch. About US$560 billion was pumped into Western banks by these funds.³ State-controlled institutions from developing and newly industrializing countries helped bail out banks in the advanced capitalist countries. This source of funds began to dry up as the funds grew increasingly wary of the spreading contagion in 2008. The banks then began to pursue potential buyers as a means of injecting the much-needed capital into their balance sheets. The Federal Reserve and Treasury essentially prodded this process along, as for instance in the buyout of Bear Stearns by Bank of America.

With the collapse of Lehman it was clear that the systemic crisis called for more drastic measures. Paul Paulson proposed the setting up of a US$700 billion fund—the Troubled Asset Relief Program (TARP) to buy up toxic assets in order to help the banks plug the holes in their balance sheets. The initial bill, a mere three pages, amounted to a blank check with no congressional oversight! After the ensuing uproar in the legislature, a revised bill, padded with US$150 billion in special tax provisions to sweeten the deal for the legislators, was passed amidst dire prognostications of economic disaster if the banks were allowed to fail. Initially, US$125 billion of TARP money was allocated to buying assets from nine major banks, a program that was christened "cash for trash."

Government purchase of assets is, however, the more inefficient way of recapitalizing the banks.⁴ The financial system was confronting a breakdown in the market for assets. As buyers fled from the market, the prices of these assets spiraled downward. The government plan to buy up these toxic assets as a way of propping up the insolvent banks was confounded by the difficulties of setting an appropriate price. Pricing the assets at the rock-bottom market prices would fail to plug the hole in a bank's balance sheet, but setting a higher price transferred the risk of the taxpayer and, in effect, absolved the banks of the consequences of their reckless investment. The scheme amounted to a state-sponsored program of a "socialization of losses and privatization of gains."

A more effective strategy that was advocated by many, including economists like Joseph Stiglitz, Paul Krugman, and Nouriel Roubini, was the direct injection of fresh capital into insolvent banks, along with a share in ownership or control. The deep aversion of the US state to any form of state intervention in markets and the strong opposition of banks to such measures meant that the US Fed Treasury was deeply resistant to rescues in the form of direct takeovers or temporary nationalization of the battered banks.

The acknowledgment that the plan to buy up the toxic assets was a nonstarter came as the approach had actually morphed into a weak recapitalization plan that set aside US$250 billion of the TARP funds for direct capital injections into failing banks. In fact, the shift in strategy came after the UK had initiated a program of direct equity infusions into British banks. With the failure of the TARP buyout scheme, Paul Paulson was forced to concede that the policy approach had to change while testifying that, "I will never apologize for changing an approach when the facts change."[5] There is an ironic echo of the famous retort attributed to Keynes: "When the facts change, I change my mind. What do you do, sir?" The context of Keynes's remark was his advocacy of official intervention in the context of the Great Depression and his evolving critique of the approach of the British Treasury and the laissez-faire orthodoxy. Paulson's recapitalization strategy remained hamstrung by his deep-seated reluctance to meddle with markets and private capital.

This was most evident in the funds that were poured into AIG. The initial US$85 billion that was pumped into AIG served essentially as a backdoor rescue of AIG creditors—the big investment banks—as the funds were funneled into making the counterparties to AIG's insurance contracts whole by covering their entire investment. These counterparty banks had taken out credit default swaps on US$62 billion worth of CDOs. The secret negotiations with the US Treasury and Federal Reserve committed the US taxpayer to buying the underlying toxic assets, paying 100 cents on the dollar without any serious attempt to ensure more favorable terms while paying AIG US$27 billion to retire the credit default swaps on these CDOs. Not only were the counterparty banks allowed to keep the US$35 billion that AIG had already paid out earlier, but there was also no serious attempt to wring concessions in the form of a discount of 10 percent on the assets as proposed by some US Federal officials. AIG also forfeited any rights to sue the banks over any irregularities with the bulk of the insured mortgage securities.[6] Goldman Sachs cornered the biggest payout of US$12.9 billion, even as its executives steadfastly maintained that they would suffer no material risk from any default by AIG! As the collateral demands on AIG continued to build, the bailout grew to US$180 billion amidst controversies over huge bonuses appropriated by AIG executives. It was later estimated that the taxpayers got back 41 cents for every dollar given, when AIG began its repayments.[7]

Half of the funds for the capital purchase program were to be invested in preferred shares of nine major banks at an interest rate of 5 percent. The banks could repurchase these shares at their own discretion at face value. The terms of the purchase reflected the government's unwillingness to assert any form of control over the private banks and also amounted to an extremely sweet deal for the banks. The absence of voting rights meant that the government had nothing to say in the subsequent running of the banks, though the banks receiving funds had to agree to accept curbs on compensation of the top executives and limit dividends. The recent rush by the rescued banks to return the TARP funds as soon as possible was prompted by this weak attempt at reining in executive pay.

Compare these terms to Warren Buffet's US$5 billion investment in Goldman Sachs at an interest rate of 10 percent, which also gave his investment fund Berkshire Hathaway more attractive warrants to buy an equivalent in common stock of Goldman Sachs—a 10 percent stake in the bank. The US taxpayer was also getting a worse deal than the British taxpayer. Under the British recapitalization scheme equity infusions of around £37 billion in the form of preference shares into British banks yielded 12 percent returns and also came with government-appointed board members.

The gyrations of the TARP did not stop here. Having evolved from an asset purchase scheme to a weak equity injection program, the next phase was to take on the onus of guaranteeing the assets in a market that continued to flounder. Additional funds of US$20 billion in the form of preference shares at an 8 percent rate of interest were allocated to Citibank and Bank of America (BOFA) apart from the earlier equity injections. In a deal announced in November 2008, the government agreed to absorb 90 percent of losses of Citibank, beyond an initial US$29 billion loss, on a portfolio of US$306 billion worth of distressed mortgage-related securities. This amounted to a total exposure of about US$235 billion. In January 2009, Bank of America was guaranteed against 90 percent losses above an initial US$10 billion on the US$118 billion pool of assets taken over from Merrill Lynch—an exposure of about US$97 billion.

The next avatar of the TARP was the Public Private Investment Partnership, mooted by Timothy Geithner, after he became the US Treasury Secretary. This program designed after consultations with big asset managers like Pimco and BlackRock, sought to encourage private investors (in particular the big asset managers who helped design the program!) to buy the toxic assets. It sweetened the deal by providing 50 percent of the equity, and then topping that through a Federal loan (or loan guarantee) of up to six times this amount! This sweetener allowed the investing bank to retain all the benefits of a rise in price, while palming off the risk of a further slide in prices on the books of the federal government and ultimately the taxpayer!

The TARP, which ended up disbursing about US$410 billion, was, however, only a small part of the money channeled by the US government into the rescue of the financial sector. A total of a whopping US$4.6 trillion was handed out to banks—32 percent of US GDP in 2008! The bigger role was played by the Federal Reserve, which, according to an estimate, provided, by far, the bulk of the funding for the bailout in the form of loans amounting to US$3.8 trillion.[8]

AT THE CENTER OF THE STORM

The Federal Reserve set up in response to the panic of 1907 had, as one of its primary functions, the role of lender of last resort. Insolvent banks could borrow funds from the Federal Reserve in order to meet liquidity and capital shortfalls. The bank failures following the Crash of 1929 paved the way for setting up the FDIC to guarantee the savings of millions of depositors. The transformation of the financial system from a deposit-based system to one based on capital markets demands a significant reorientation of the mechanisms the Federal Reserve uses to provide liquidity and restore stability. While in the earlier institutional setting the Federal Reserve's discount rate was a key instrument in regulating the flow of liquidity, liquidity and credit creation now depend more fundamentally on buying and selling capital assets by the security dealers.[9] These dealings have fostered a parallel private and unregulated monetary mechanism outside the ambit of control of the central bank.

The real problem for central bank policy was the failure of the various measures to revive lending by pumping liquidity into the financial system and coaxing banks into lending through transfusions of capital to restore the broken credit machinery. Financial institutions remained wary of lending to anyone other than the government. The flows into the Federal Funds market dwindled as a consequence, since banks have a greater incentive to stockpile reserves rather than lend to other banks. Restoring credit may have been the Fed's primary aim, but it was also groping its way toward finding means to reassert control over the collapsing markets and resort to a more "unconventional" monetary strategy. A critical part of this response to the crisis was the agenda of reestablishing the control of the US Fed over the international financial system. To do so, the Federal Reserve began intervening across a wider range of asset markets.[10]

The Crisis of 2008 saw a disruption of funding liquidity in the money market getting transformed into the breakdown of market liquidity in capital market. As money market mutual funds stopped buying the asset-backed commercial paper of the shadow banking system, they turned to banks to provide a credit line. Banks in turn took resort to eurodollar markets driving up the rates at which banks lent to each other in this market (the London Interbank Offered Rate (LIBOR) rate) relative to the rate at which banks lent to each other in the US market. As this difference—the Treasury and Eurodollar Deposit (TED) spread—spiked, the Fed had to step in to provide a backstop and widen lending.[11]

After the Bear Stearns's debacle, the Federal extended its discount window to the failing investment banks. Apart from boosting its Term Auction Facilities under which it offered funds to depository institutions, the Fed announced the setting up of the Term Securities Lending Facility through which it would begin to lend treasuries for up to 28 days against investment grade assets to primary dealers. These treasuries could be used as collateral in repurchase agreements, in effect helping to liquefy the bank's balance sheets. Liquidity support was also provided through Central Bank swap lines—the arrangements under which banks exchange currency.

By September 2008, when the subprime collapse had grown into a full-blown crisis, it was clear that the sale of treasuries bills would not be adequate to meet the surging demand for funds. The seizure of the credit markets meant that this bloated monetary base was being hoarded in the form of excess reserves posted by the banks at the Federal Reserve. From normal levels of around US$7 billion, these reserves deposited were pushing toward US$1 trillion and excess reserves climbed to roughly 10 percent of total bank assets.[12]

The Federal Reserve sought ways to restore the markets for securities through purchases of mortgage-backed securities and securities backed by credit card auto and student loans. To this end, the Fed set up the Term Asset-Backed Securities Lending Facility to buy asset-backed securities and also an SPV under the Commercial Paper Funding Facility to buy commercial paper issued by financial institutions.

In effect, the Federal Reserve has been attempting to establish itself as the market maker of last resort—intervening to stem the tide when the private broker dealer system threatened to implode.[13] It has been doing so in two essential ways: first, as a buyer of a wide range of distressed toxic assets of the shadow banking system that cannot find a price or a market in the current turbulent times and second, by lending against a wide range of illiquid private sector securities. This can be seen if we look at the asset side of the balance sheet of the Federal Reserve, in particular, in the sharp expansion and the diversification of holding primarily treasury securities that can be seen since September 2008 (Figure 4.1). The share of treasuries in this ballooning balance sheets declined from 90 to 21 percent as the Fed acquired more unconventional assets including mortgage-backed securities and commercial paper under its liquidity programs like the Term Auction Facilities.

Figure 4.1. Federal Reserve Balance Sheet (Assets): Market Maker of Last Resort (US$ Billion)

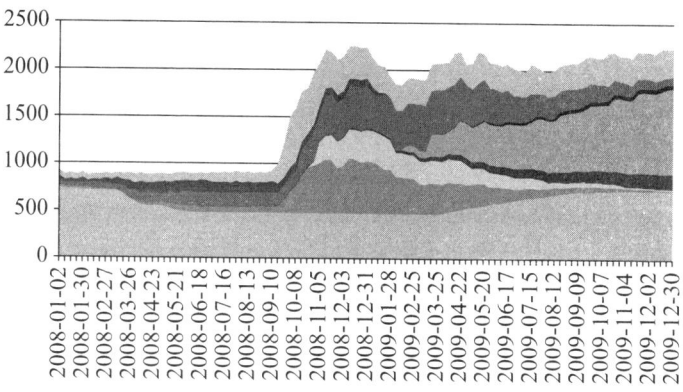

- Treasury Securities
- Commercial Paper Funding Facility
- Mortgage-backed securities
- Term auction Facility
- Other
- Central Bank Liquidity Swaps
- Agency Debt
- Term Asset-Backed Securities Loan Facility
- Repurchase

Source: Federal Reserve.

In a context where the private security dealer had emerged as a key player in liquidity and credit creation, the crisis highlighted the fact that, when it came to the crunch, the system needed the state to step into the breach. Before the crisis, the shadow banking system had funded securitization with money market funds that mobilized private savings. As the crisis unfolded, it was the Federal Reserve that moved in to fund the securitization machine by expanding its reserve liabilities by borrowing from the treasury (Figure 4.2).[14] It also extended debt guarantees to a wider range

Figure 4.2. Federal Reserve Balance Sheet (Liabilities): Quantitative Easing (US$ Billion)

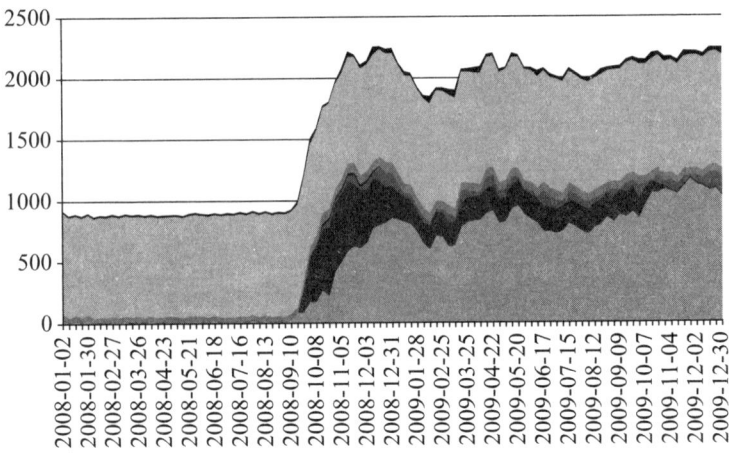

- Reserve balances with Federal Reserve Banks
- Treasury, general account
- Reverse repurchase agreements: Foreign
- Other
- Treasury, supplementary financing account
- Reverse repurchase agreements: Dealers
- Currency in circulation

Source: Federal Reserve.

of assets enabling financial institutions to raise money by selling bonds to private investors backed by this guarantee.

The conception is that if the securitization mechanisms are facing a threat, the resolution requires the central bank stepping in as a guarantor or insurer of these beleaguered securities. The various liquidity programs are effectively attempting to place a floor below the downward spiral of asset prices. This is analogous to the Federal role in insuring private deposits. The central bank is emerging as the final bulwark of the credit machinery driven by capital markets, mopping up surplus funds that the banks are wary of lending and providing liquidity to institutions facing funding shortfalls.

This is what has been called the policy of quantitative easing. Quantitative easing, or credit easing, as Bernanke's preferred term for the policy can be viewed as the funding counterpart of the Fed's role as the dealer of last resort not only in the money market but more fundamentally in the capital market as a whole. The Federal Reserve funded its interventions not just by the sale of treasury securities but increasingly by expanding its reserve liabilities by borrowing from the treasury (Figure 4.2).[15]

One implication of this policy is that the Fed's balance sheet has expanded almost without limit. The Fed had about a US$800 billion balance sheet to operate in a US$50 trillion credit market before the crisis. Its balance sheet rose from US$874 billion in August 2007 to US$900 billion before the fall of Lehman. Since then, it has surged to about US$2.2 trillion (on December 11, 2008) over just a few months. It soared to nearly US$3 trillion by 2010.

Unlike Japan, which had also pumped up its balance sheet (between 2001 and 2006) to revive its economy, the Fed policy under Bernanke has not been restricted to the purchase of government securities but has as we have seen taken a wider range of financial assets out of the system, and is also *greater in magnitude* than that implemented by the Bank of Japan.[16]

By conjuring more than US$2 trillion of stimulus out of thin air, the Federal Reserve took on even more credit risk while purchasing illiquid private assets. If the unconventional monetary policy works, with the economy picking up and the return of inflation, the Federal Reserve will come under pressure to sell assets into the market, to mop up the excess money it has created in fighting deflation—a pressure that would be exacerbated in the face of burgeoning public debt. With the aggressive expansion of the Federal Reserve balance sheet and the ramping up of treasury issuance, the market for treasuries will be deluged. Right now these treasuries are a globally sought safe haven, but once confidence is restored to the credit markets, funds would seek out higher returns and flee the markets. Given that foreign holdings represent a significant proportion of the stockholdings of US treasuries, the collapse in treasury prices would manifest itself in a collapse of the US dollar as inflation soars and foreign demand for treasuries flags.[17]

In a sense this policy was, in fact, an invitation to investors to bet the policy will fail and the slump would persist, so that interest rates remain on the floor. By reassuring investors that it would hold overnight lending rates at near zero for the foreseeable future, the Federal Reserve essentially gave traders an extremely cheap way to borrow overnight and invest the proceeds in higher yielding assets. The implicit hope was that the increased borrowing would be used to purchase higher risk financial assets and restart the securities markets inside the US (as well as financing higher levels of consumer spending and business investment). In other words, foster another bubble![18]

This strategy in no way aimed to check the juggernaut of reckless speculation that fed the securitization frenzy. More so, because, even as the state has been taking on the onus in financing and guaranteeing the private financial system, it has not expended equivalent initiative in fine-tuning and developing a regulatory apparatus to curb speculative excess in a rapidly evolving financial system. On the contrary, it has been following a course of dismantling and eroding the regulatory controls that had been put in place in the aftermath of the Great Depression. There has been a ratcheting up of state support of the banking system not just over the past three years or even the past few decades but over the past century as the state widened the scope of its safety net to cover liquidity, deposit, and capital insurance needs of the financial system.[19] This bulging safety net, however, stokes even greater speculative and risk-taking behavior. So the potential cost of crises in the future keeps snowballing—what has been called the "doom loop."[20] Government interventions by rescuing banks from their follies in order to restore stability, in effect, revive and reinvigorate the speculative juggernaut.

In the aftermath of the crisis, the need for regulation has been widely acknowledged. But the contrast in the manner in which the bank rescues were pushed through and the slow and protracted path of the initiatives to reform the financial sector suggests that, genie of finance, once unleashed, is not easily tamed.

PUTTING THE GENIE BACK INTO THE BOTTLE

Regulatory policy in the past decades has been dominated by the dogma that finance is best equipped to police itself. The separation of commercial and investment banking enshrined in the

77

Glass–Steagall Act had been gradually eroded, in particular, by the move to raise the share of incomes banks were allowed from security trading up from 10 percent to a quarter of earnings. The process has been further boosted by the systematic measures that eased the path for banks seeking to expand and diversify into new activities.

This meant that the Fed guarantee of deposit-taking institutions was in effect extended to securities and trading operations. In 1994, when a wave of derivative scandals prompted the US Congress to consider measures to regulate the booming derivatives trades, the major banks in coordination with the International Swaps and Derivatives Association (ISDA) launched a concerted campaign to resist any form of regulatory oversight in favor of an internal monitoring system, insisting that the banks could be trusted to regulate themselves![21] The incipient attempts to regulate the derivatives industry were shelved, and four years later, when Brooksley Born, the then chair of the Commodity Futures Trading Commission warned about the buildup of huge over-the-counter derivative positions and pressed for some regulatory controls, she was silenced by the Clinton team of Greenspan, Rubin, and Summers and a moratorium on regulatory action by the commission was imposed. In 1997, when the Commodities Futures Trading Commission proposed regulating interest and currency swaps, ISDA lobbied and defeated this proposal. The Commodity Futures Modernization Act introduced in 1999 finally exempted derivatives from federal regulation.

At the same time banks began to aggressively use securitization and credit default swaps to reduce capital requirements and increase leverage. In 2001, regulatory authorities loosened the rules for assessing capital requirements by introducing measurement rules based on credit ratings for asset-backed securities. This facilitated the lowering of the capital–asset ratio through financial engineering, and further cemented the cozy relationship between the debt watchdogs—the ratings companies—and the bank. A few years later in 2004, the five major investment banks including Goldman Sachs with Paulson at the helm extracted an agreement that allowed them to use their internal computer models to calculate net capital in their brokerage units. The relaxation of the rules, essentially handed back the job of monitoring risk to the banks themselves, giving them greater leeway to stretch leverage. The new powers that the SEC extracted to monitor the books of these banks, in return for this loosening of regulation, were never exercised, despite numerous red flags being raised about excessive leverage and other risk factors. Deregulation and the low interest rate regime put in place under Alan Greenspan have been conducive to the growth of the shadow banking system and to the reckless pursuit of leverage and returns that led to the bubble.

In the wake of the crisis, this laissez-faire approach came into question. The sanctity of the models that the wizards of finance had constructed as a proxy for markets has been shown to be illusory. There has been a growing pressure to bring trade in over-the-counter derivatives and swaps out in the open into centralized clearing houses and exchanges where there would be greater transparency, market discovery, and guarantors on both sides of the contract. Given that, by 2009, the five largest banks controlled 95 percent of the market for derivatives,[22] there was a strong opposition by the banks to provisions in the financial reform bill that sought to assert control and oversight on such trades. The provision proposed by Senator Blanche Lincoln to force banks to spin off swap and derivative trading desks into separate entities was shelved from the Wall Street Reform and Consumer Protection Act—popularly called the Dodd–Frank

Act—that was finally passed in July 2010, and the proposal for steering these instruments through a centralized exchange was watered down to exempt many customized contracts. In a stab at reining in speculative derivative trading, a provision in the act forces banks to retain 5 percent of all classes of securities issued on their books to ensure that they have a stake or what is called some "skin in the game."

The other major overhaul is the resurrection of a Glass–Steagall style insulation of government-insured investor deposits from reckless speculative behavior of banks in the form of the Volcker rule. Under this rule, banks were to be banned from owning hedge funds, private equity groups, or proprietary trading units. The principle behind the ban on proprietary trading by banks (the modern version of the separation of commercial and investment banking) was to keep trading on behalf of customers separate from trading by such funds for their own profit. Such a firewall would also address the conflict of interest implicit in bankers promoting certain trades and investments of clients while undertaking bets against these trades with their own capital. The final version exempts insurance and mutual fund companies from the bar on proprietary trading, while allowing banks to invest up to 3 percent of their capital in private equity and hedge funds instead of a blanket ban on such trades.

The other important plank of the reforms that have been pushed through in the US is the setting up of the Financial Stability Oversight Council as a new "orderly liquidation authority," which gives regulators the power to identify and seize a failing "systemically important" institution, pare off the vulnerable parts, sack executives, and use the assets to pay creditors while imposing haircuts or losses on them. Institutions that are too big to fail would no longer depend on the largesse or safety net of a government guarantee.

This ambitious proposal seeks to end the AIG-type bailouts or Lehman-style bankruptcy that wreaked such havoc on the financial system. The ultimate oversight for this resolution authority would rest with the Federal Deposit Insurance Corporation. The proposal to levy fees totaling US$19 billion on banks with more than US$50 billion in assets was finally scrapped to ensure the passage of the bill, so the winding down of failing institutions will now be financed by higher FDIC fees and the sleight of hand of an early termination of the state authority to use TARP funds. Further, the role of the resolution authority would also be restricted solely to domestic operations.

The idea is to prevent institutions that are too big to fail holding the government hostage. A crucial bit of the legislation—the Kanjorwski amendment—grants regulators the power to break up a financial institution if it posed a risk to the financial system. In discussion on limits on the size of banks, proposals putting a cap of 10 percent of the total of deposit liabilities and 3 percent cap of all non-deposit liabilities have been suggested. Other proposals place limits in terms of share of GDP. The issue of size becomes more important in the context of the intensifying global concentration in the sector. In 1998, the five largest banks owned 8 percent of global assets, but by 2008 their share had doubled to 16 percent. In the US, the total assets of the top three banks as a share of commercial banking assets rose from 10 percent in 1990 to more than 40 percent after the crises. Political influence of Wall Street nurtured the laissez-faire approach that further catalyzed the growth and concentration of the banking sector.[23] The structure of the industry in the aftermath of the crisis is even more highly concentrated.

The problem is not simply that of size, though size and concentration strengthen the power and influence these institutions wield. The more vexed issue is that of interconnectedness—the rapid speed of the spread of contagion in a tightly integrated financial market. After all, the Great Depression witnessed the failure of numerous small banks. The financial system's propensity to generate fragility cannot be curbed simply by pruning banks down to size. Finance also has a way of innovating means to evade and preempt regulatory controls in its pursuit of profits. In this context, the proposals like the Volker rule or the proposal to limit government guarantees solely to institutions that perform the original functions of finance—that of mobilizing savings and channeling these to the most productive uses—so-called utility banking, [24] seek to separate the casino aspects of finance from its more productive roles, and ensure that the public safety net does not end up promoting speculative activities. The advocacy of limited purpose banking that transforms banks, insurance companies, hedge funds, etc., into fully transparent mutual fund companies pursues a similar path.[25]

Finance is, however, not easily contained. Not only is the belief that regulation can contain speculation misguided, the notion that a firewall can be erected around the "useful" or productive parts of finance is also like chasing a will of the wisp. Historically, the lines between commercial and investment banking have been blurred by the emergence of huge universal banks. In practice, the Volcker Rule is likely to be equally hard to enforce. The same innovations that have been central to finance's "productive" role in mobilizing savings, promoting investment, and managing risk also give rise to the speculative booms. There is a danger in focusing only on the failure of regulation or the regulatory capture of the state by finance. Such a focus evades the confrontation with the deeper structural problems that gave rise to the crisis.

PUMPED BY DEBT, STARVED FOR JOBS

In particular, the excessive private debt of leveraged households formed the grounds for the rich pickings of the financial sector. This burgeoning debt has also been the primary force supporting demand in the US economy through the past few recessions. If the housing bubble restarted the economy after the bust of the dot-com boom, the dot-com boom of the 1990s was itself an antidote to the recession that followed the savings and loans debacle. Greenspan's response to each debt-induced crisis—the famed "Greenspan Put" that lowered interest rates—reignited asset speculation driving recovery by stoking even more debt. In fact the Federal Reserve's interventions since the Crash of 1987 have unleashed a series of debt-fueled booms and busts, culminating in the current crisis. The contribution of rising debt levels to demand and economic activity in the US has been substantial.[26]

If the rising debt levels drove demand in the economy during boom times, deleveraging or the unwinding of debt in the private sector during the collapse precipitated a contraction of demand. With the fizzling out of debt demand during the downturn, unemployment rose. Unemployment has risen from a precrisis level of around 4.5 percent in 2007 to 10 percent in 2009 as a result of debt deflation. This figure does not measure the full extent of the problem since it does not take into account workers who have dropped out of the workforce after a long and unsuccessful search for employment, or part-time workers who would snap up a full time job, if available. The broader measure of unemployment that includes discouraged workers and involuntary part-time workers was as much as 17.5 percent in 2009.[27]

The lesson Keynes drew from the Great Depression was that, when markets fail and investor confidence stalls the economic engine, the state can fill the breach and pump prime the economy through public spending. As fears of another Great Depression stalked policy makers across the globe, the Keynesian doctrine that had been pushed into cold storage for some decades regained a following as governments around the globe began to implement stimulus packages to revive spending.

In the US under Bush, the favored form of stimulus was tax cuts, which redistributed wealth toward the already wealthy. This was the approach followed during the recession in 2001. Such an approach does not, however, yield dividends in terms of job creation. Two years into the recovery, GDP grew at an average rate of 3.4 percent but the rate of job growth declined by around 1.8 percent. The problem is in fact even deeper. The recession in the early 1990s was also characterized by a jobless recovery with job losses of 1.4 percent in the 27-month period after the low point of unemployment.[28] Two years down the road from the crunch of 2008, it is clear that the US is headed for a third jobless recovery (Figure 4.3).

The lopsided nature of the previous recoveries has exacerbated the trauma of joblessness in the current crisis. The structure of job opportunities in the US has become sharply polarized over the past two decades, with job opportunities expanding at one end in high-skill, high-wage occupations and at the other end in low-skill, low-wage occupations. This polarization has become even more so after the crisis with middle-wage, middle-skill white-collar and blue-collar jobs getting squeezed even further.[29] The unemployment rate is comparable to that in 1980, but joblessness is increasingly concentrated among the long-term unemployed and underemployed, who are gradually dropping out of the labor force after staying unemployed for longer periods of time compared to the 1980s' recession. Of the 14.6 million unemployed in the US

Figure 4.3. New Nonfarm Payroll Jobs (Month on Month) (Thousands)

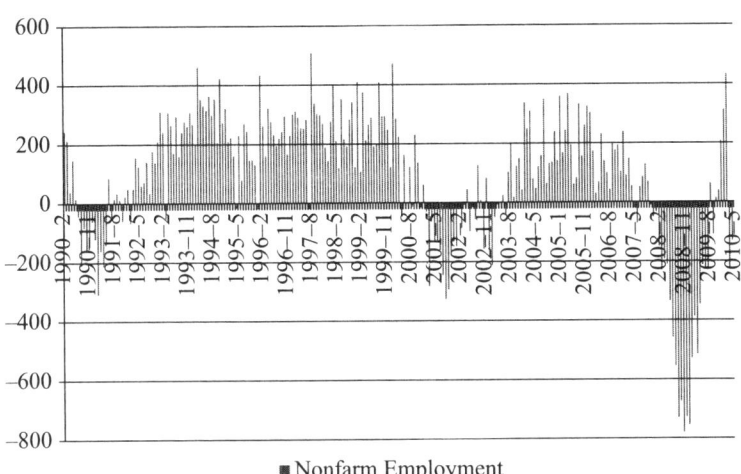

■ Nonfarm Employment

Source: Bureau of Labor Statistics.

in July 2010, around 1.4 million have been out of a job for more than 99 weeks, the point at which unemployment benefits run out. There are about another 8.5 million who are working part time but need full-time jobs. And finally there are about 3.9 million missing workers who have dropped out of the workforce.[30] Of today's unemployed workers, 45 percent have been without a job for more than 26 weeks. This share has not exceeded 26 percent in any downturn in the postwar period.[31] These are the workers who would, in the normal course, no longer be eligible for unemployment benefits, which ran out after 26 weeks, before unemployment benefits were extended in face of the these recession.

The stimulus package that Obama pushed through after much wrangling was set to pump around US$787 billion into the economy over two years and stem the tide of joblessness. While one-third of this went to tax cuts to business, the remaining two-thirds was to be spent on meeting budget shortfalls in state and local governments (a significant employer), funding for Medicaid green initiatives, and "shovel ready" infrastructure projects. At around 2 percent of GDP, this stimulus could hardly counteract the deflationary consequences of the fizzling out of the debt-fueled boom. Debt had contributed more than 25 percent of aggregate expenditure (adding US$4.7 trillion to aggregate spending compared to an annual GDP of US$14 trillion) before the collapse, compared to a contribution of 2 percent in 1954.[32]

In September 2010, the number of payroll jobs fell short of the pre-level rate by around 8.1 million jobs. If one adds to this an estimated 3.4 million new job seekers, the job's gap was about 11.5 million jobs.[33] With about six job seekers for every new job in 2009, down to about five job seekers in the middle of 2010, the job market shows no signs of easing and the private sector job creation is picking up only at a glacial pace.[34] The drop in hiring has been more important than actual layoffs in the jobless recovery. This flagging rate of job creation, despite the slight recovery of output, pervades all industrial sectors to different degrees.[35]

The grim prospect of long-term unemployment—what is now being billed as the "new normal" that the US has to get used to—is one that policy response is failing to come to grips with. The tortuous passage of the stimulus bill contrasts sharply with the ramming through of the TARP bill. It was after weeks of stalling that the move to renew the provision temporarily extending unemployment benefits from the 26-week limit up to 66 to 99 weeks was finally passed. While providing some relief, this left the 1.4 million long-term jobless out in the lurch. The US$200 billion job's bill that Obama had proposed was watered down in both the Senate and House versions. The provision to pump an additional US$50 billion into the beleaguered state budgets, including pay for a thousands of school teachers, was finally passed in the summer of 2010 after being pared down to a mere US$26 billion.

While around US$4.6 trillion was pumped into the banks that had through their relentless pursuit of returns laid the grounds for the implosion, initiatives at directly creating jobs have been stymied by raising the bogey of rising deficits. The moves to give relief to those facing foreclosures and give bankruptcy courts the power to rework mortgages have been impeded and derailed.

THE REIGN OF WALL STREET

This is not simply the clash of a Keynesian and a Friedmanite worldview with the former cautioning against the risk of market failure and a deflationary crisis and the latter stressing the fundamental buoyancy of markets as long as the economy was kept flush with money during such a crisis. In the diametrically opposite focus on creating and protecting jobs and livelihoods through direct public investments, on the one hand, and in creating conditions where finance and private capital are given sufficient incentives to resume lending and investment on the other, there is a fundamental reflection of class interest and alignment. The overwhelming preoccupation has been with restoring the fortunes of finance even when it was clear that the real suffering was among those facing the loss of jobs and homes.

This is clear in the very different tack taken toward the auto industry. Around US$60 billion were provided to General Motors and Chrysler while pushing them through their bankruptcy proceedings. However, in contrast to the bank rescues which displayed a signal reluctance to assert any form of control over banks, the auto industry was forced to accept stringent terms and conditions, with significant sacrifices being thrust on workers who had to sign off future pay hikes and benefits and accept a major restructuring of jobs. Repeated and misleading assertions of the overpaid workers earning US$70 an hour[36] (a figure that conveniently includes the pensions and benefits of currently retired workers) helped spread the perception that the auto industries' problems were due to these overpaid workers. While the significant services rendered by bankers were being extolled in defense of the bailouts of their institutions and the huge bonuses they had cornered through the crisis, huge concessions were extracted from one of the important trade unions in the US, the United Autoworkers Union, as a condition for the rescue of the auto industry.

One of the last bastions of the blue-collar worker came under assault, while the bankers came out relatively unscathed and with their hubris intact. A case in point is the tale of Andrew Hall, head of Phibro, the oil-trading unit of Citigroup. Having come under fire for a huge nine-figure bonus given to Hall, Citigroup decided to offload the unit to Occidental, rather than accept the government curbs on pay. And so Andrew Hall got to keep his US$98 million bonus, since his new employer did not come under the radar of the pay restrictions![37]

The Financial Crisis Inquiry Commission headed by Phil Angelides has turned the spotlight on some of the worst excesses of the banking sector and the recent indictment of Goldman Sachs by the SEC could potentially open the flood gates of litigation against the banking sector. So far, those who had steered the economy on its disastrous course remain exempt from any real liability for the consequences. Already the Supreme Court in a recent judgment raised doubt about the definition of fraud in the case of the notorious Enron chief, Jeffrey Skilling, and the leaders of the financial industry continue to maintain that what they did was not fraudulent or criminal but the normal conduct of business among sophisticated investors. It might be true as Senator Kaufman bemoaned "fraud and potential criminal conduct were at the heart of the financial crisis." However, the actions of Wall Street brokers have to be viewed in the context of the industry norms and practices that had been set in place. The seeds of the crisis were not sown by the Ponzi schemes of Bernie Madoff, but the everyday money-raking transactions on Wall Street that fueled the bubble.

Two years after the collapse, finance bounced right back, while workers and the poor in America continue to struggle, the Economic Policy Institute has a revealing graphic that brings this disparity into sharp focus. Corporate profits sustained a huge hit through 2008, but recovered by the first quarter of 2010 to a level that was 5.7 percent higher than its level in the last quarter of 2007. The number of jobs has fallen by 5.9 percent over the same period—around 8.2 million jobs have been lost.[38] In part, the reason could lie in the US$5 billion the financial industry as a whole spent on lobbying and campaign funding between 1998 and 2008. Finance is the second biggest source of campaign contributions after the healthcare industry. Subprime lenders and the major banks that financed their activities were responsible for funneling about US$370 million of this money. As the pressure for financial reform grew, and the Obama government mooted proposals for tightening regulatory structure, these banks switched from funding both democrats and republicans to pouring money increasingly to the republicans to stymie the passage of these proposals (Figure 4.4)![39]

Even beyond such extensive lobbying, the sway of finance has been buttressed by the "revolving door" between the government and finance, the hopping of persons from key posts in major banks and government. The deep ties and interpenetration between the

Figure 4.4. Jobs and Profits in the US

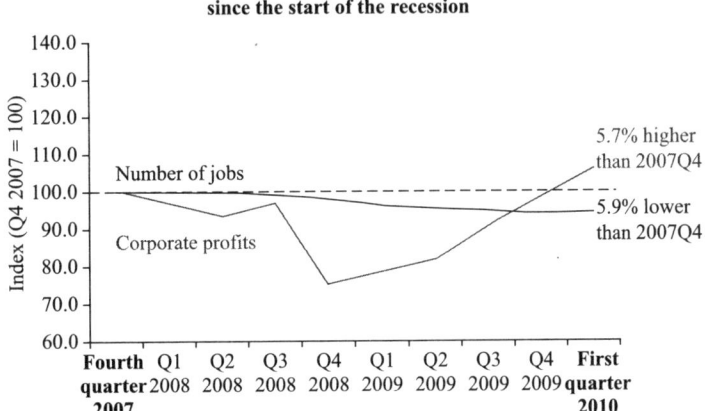

**Change in corporate profits and number of jobs in the US
since the start of the recession**

Source: Economic Policy Institute (http://www.epi.org/page/-/img/071410-snapshot.jpg).

Note: Profits reflect total profits of all companies doing business in the US as well as earnings of US companies abroad.

government executive branch, the Federal Reserve, the treasury, and the financial sector forged a common worldview that subserves the imperatives of finance and the neoliberal distaste for hindering, in any way, their forage for profits. The financial oligarchy is deeply embedded in the structure of state power. It is not for nothing that the contemporary take on the old saying, "what is good for GM is good for America" is "what is good for Goldman is good for America."

This cozy nexus, where the financial and corporate capital and state power buttress each other, was central to the rise of the neoliberal orthodoxy that laid the seeds of the crisis.[40] If we focus simply on instruments like the notorious credit default swaps, or on the huge regulatory gaps that skewed the incentive structure, we miss the larger picture. Even beyond the proximate causes for the profligate binge of the last decade, the crisis is rooted in the realignment of social forces after the stagflation of the 1970s. The balance of class forces that emerged in this process set the juggernaut of financialization loose, and unleashed the specific dynamic of accumulation that characterized the neoliberal period.

Chapter 5

Another Gilded Age

> We are doing God's work.... We are very important. We help companies grow by helping them raise capital. Companies create wealth. This in turn allows people to have jobs that create more growth and more wealth. We have a social purpose.
>
> — Lloyd Blankfein, CEO, Goldman Sachs, *Sunday Times*, November 8, 2009

Financialization has been characterized as the "pattern of accumulation in which profit making occurs increasingly through financial channels rather than through trade and commodity production."[1] Financialization is, however, much more than the mere proliferation of financial instruments. It reflects the growing political and economic power of finance in recent decades. At the heart of this development is the neoliberal revolution that celebrated the efficacy of markets and sought to give a free rein to the logic of profit seeking. This revolution is not simply a revival of a laissez-faire doctrine. It is more fundamentally about the capture and harnessing of state power in the service, the interests and priorities of finance, and corporate capital. Neoliberal ideology and the neoliberal policy were deployed to systematically shift the balance of power in favor of corporate and financial capital and to redistribute wealth in their favor. The roots of the current crisis lie in this structural transformation that enabled the rise to dominance of finance after the stagflation of the 1970s.

THE COUP OF FINANCE

In the 1970s and 1980s, the fight against inflation became a tool for restructuring class relations in the US. Paul Volcker, the chairman of the Federal Reserve initiated a program of monetary austerity, sharply raising interest rates from around 7.5 percent to over 20 percent in 1979. This interest hike of 1979—the Volcker shock— was a pivotal moment paving the way for what can be called "the coup of finance."[2] The Keynesian policy prescriptions of welfare and public spending to boost the economy fell into disrepute. In its stead, the emerging neoliberal policy consensus shifted in favor of rolling back state interventions to regulate or manage markets and prices and establishing the priority of policies favorable to corporate and financial profitability.

Finance capital began to push back against the regulatory framework in its quest for returns. The Depository Institutions and Deregulation and Monetary Control Act of 1980 phased out "Regulation Q" that placed a ceiling on interest rates paid out on deposits. It also broadened the powers of thrift institutions and raised the deposit insurance limits to US$100,000. The clampdown on inflation and the abolition of fixed fee commissions in 1975 pushed investment banks into searching out new avenues of profit. The successive easing of financial regulations in the USA through the 1980s and 1990s culminating in the Gramm–Leach– Bliley Bank Reform Act, 1999 (that brought to an end the legal separation of commercial banking and investment functions in financial institutions) gradually dismantled the regulatory structure that had been put in place in response to the Great Depression. Finance emerged as a powerful force shaping the economic structure of the US economy.

A simple measure of the growing importance of finance is its rising share in national income. Financial assets were less than five times the size of the US GDP in 1980, but by 2007 these had grown to over 10 times US GDP. US credit market debt rose to a level of over 3.5 times GDP by 2007 from a level of about 1.6 times GDP in 1973 (Figure 5.1). A second indicator is the increasing significance of the profits of the financial sector in overall corporate profits. The share of financial sector profits in total corporate profits increased from a low of around 12 percent in 1985 to peak at 40 percent in 2003. The share fell to 27 percent in 2008, but has resumed its upward trend in 2009 (Figure 5.2).

Figure 5.1. Financial Assets and Debt (As a Ratio of GDP)

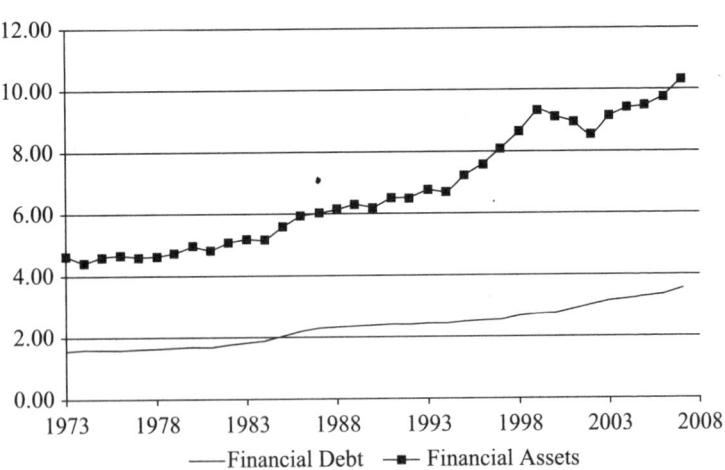

Source: Bureau of Economic Analysis.

Figure 5.2. Financial Sector Profits (As a Percentage Share of Total Corporate Profits)

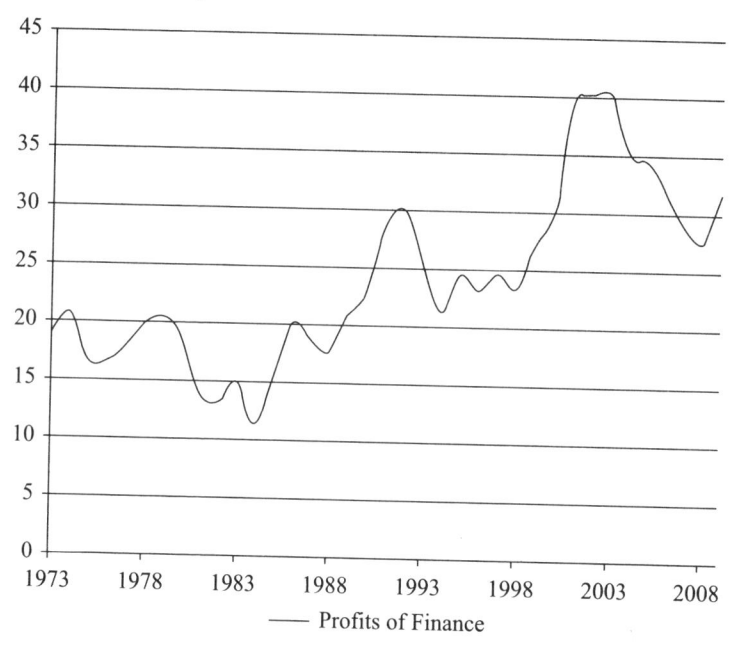

— Profits of Finance

Source: National Income and Production Accounts.

Deregulation fueled a wave of mergers and acquisitions, aggressive financial innovations, and strategies of greater risk taking described earlier. With the growth of securitization, noninterest income began rising relative to interest income. Bank earnings became less dependent on the business of borrowing at a low interest rate and then lending out at a higher rate, but rather derived increasingly from using the cheap money to churn out exotic products in return for fees and commissions. Low interest rates were no longer a constraint on bank earnings. Commercial banks have seen the share of noninterest income rise from less than 10 percent of bank revenue in the early 1980s to more than 50 percent by 2005. Large banks in particular became increasingly geared to noninterest earnings. Citigroup reported noninterest income equal to 52 percent of adjusted operating income in 2005, while JPMorgan Chase reported 64 percent of its income in a noninterest form.[3]

The business of securitization did not just boost financial sector profits through this period. It also led to the incredible enrichment of banking executives. As the banks kept cranking out financial products, the bankers brokering these deals gathered huge bonuses. The bonuses that the CEOs of bailed out Wall Street banks cornered caused a huge outrage after the banks began to teeter and collapse, but these bonuses were part of a wider trend. The Wall Street bonus pool, which hovered around 2.2 billion before 1990, surged to nearly US$35 billion in 2006. The average bonus of mangers within this pool rose from US$14,000 to a peak of US$191,000 in 2006 (Figure 5.3).

Figure 5.3. Average Wall Street Bonus (US$000)

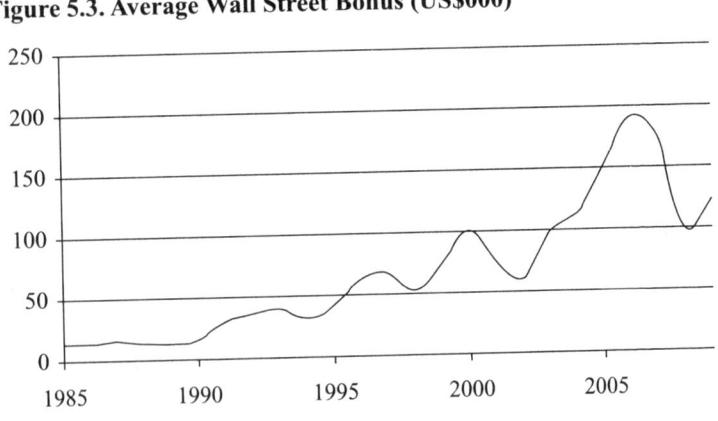

Source: Office of the State Comptroller, New York City Securities Industry Bonus Pool.

The structural shift is even more evident in the way compensation paid to bankers has evolved. The financial sector enjoys a wage premium with respect to other sectors. This premium is far in excess of any returns to education, skill intensity, and unemployment risk factors. This excess wage can be measured as the difference of the ratio of the wage of the financial sector relative to the nonfarm private sector and ratio of a benchmark relative wage based on what bankers could expect to earn above the nonfarm private sector on the basis of their relatively higher educational and skill levels (Figure 5.4).[4] This premium has risen significantly since the 1990s fueled by the flurry of innovations in the financial sector. By 2005 this premium was about 0.4 or 40 percent, implying that a banker could expect to earn 40 percent more than the wage of other workers over and above what you would expect them to earn, based on skills and education. It is, in a sense, a rent

Figure 5.4. Excess Wages in Finance (As Share of Wages of Other Workers)

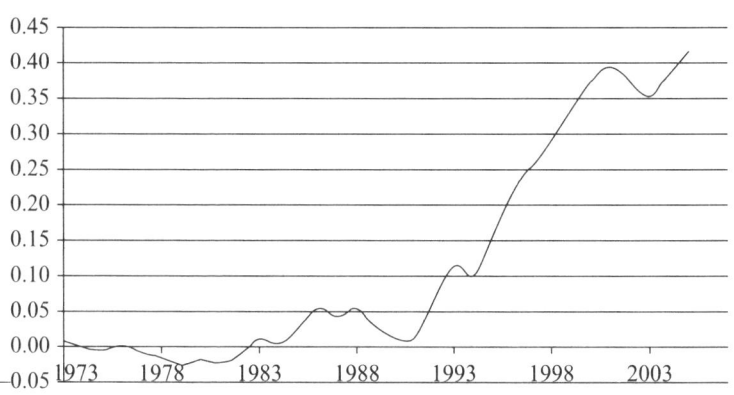

——Excess Wage in Finance

Source: Phillipon and Resheff. 2009. Wages and Human Capital in the US Banking Industry: 1909–2006." NBER Working Paper 14644.

extracted by the bankers, who, in the brave new world of structured finance, wield their monopoly over the arcane workings of this world to claim huge cuts of the bank earnings (Figure 5.4).

There was a wider process at work. Executive pay throughout the corporate sector surged through this period. Salaries and compensation for the highest paid CEOs from the Forbes list have risen significantly since the 1990s. Average CEO compensation (for the top 100 CEOs), including stock options exercised, jumped from 38 times to 768 times the average wage of a full-time worker in 2005 (Figure 5.5). This growing divergence between CEO salary and that of the average worker is also evident if we look at the

Figure 5.5. Average Salaries of Top 100 CEOs (As a Ratio of Average Wage in US$2,000)

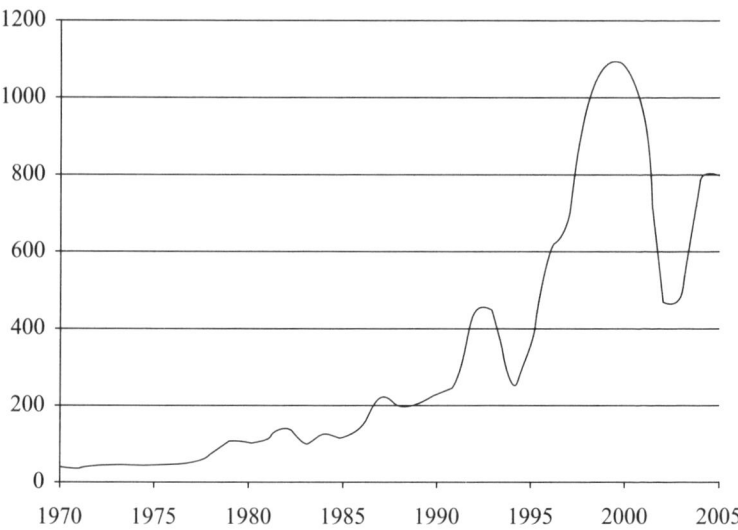

Source: Piketty, T. and E. Saez. 2007. "Income and Wage Inequality in the US: 1913–2002" in A.B. Atkinson and T. Piketty (eds), *Top Incomes over the Twentieth Century*, Available at http://elsa.berkeley.edu/~saez/piketty-saezOUP04US.pdf.

ratio of the average compensation of the major 350 public companies (reported by the Wall Street Journal/Mercer-Hay group) and the nonsupervisory production worker's pay. This ratio rose from 35 in 1978 to 298 at the end of the recovery in 2000. After a fall during the dot-com bust, it recovered to 275 times that of the typical worker by 2007. In other words, in 2007 a CEO earned more in one workday than what the typical worker earned all year.[5]

GROWING INEQUALITY AND THE WAR ON LABOR

As a result of this growing divergence in earnings, there has been a significant increase in inequality since finance launched its coup in 1979. The dominance of finance and the neoliberal ideology fueled the extraordinary enrichment of the top echelons of US society. Income was redistributed away from workers as wages were squeezed and hefty earnings were made from financial speculation, proprietary trading, and risk arbitrage.[6]

The share of the top 10 percent of the income earners rose from around 33 percent of total income in the 1970s to nearly 50 percent in 2007.[7] The picture is even starker if the spotlight is turned on the top 1 percent of the population who received nearly 18 percent of the national after-tax income in 2006 more than double their 8 percent share in 1979.[8] This group received nearly 73 times as much in average after-tax income as the bottom one-fifth of households in 2006, more than tripling the rich–poor gap in less than three decades since 1979, when the richest households made 23 times as much as the poorest households.[9] The income of the top 1 percent rose by more than 250 percent, while that of the bottom 20 percent rose by around 10 percent in the period 1979–2006 (Figure 5.6).

Figure 5.6 Increase in Income 1979–2006

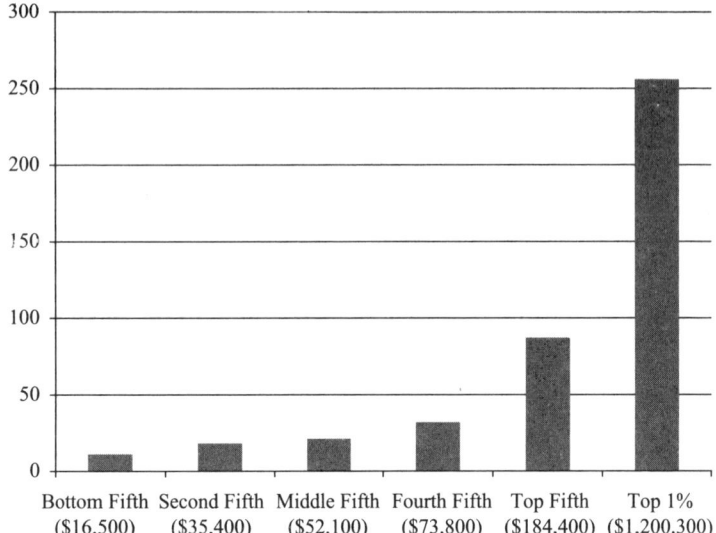

Source: Sherman, A. 2009. *Income Gaps Hit Record Levels. In 2006: New Data Show Rich-Poor Gap Tripled Between 1979 and 2006.* Center on Budget and Policy Priorities.

The share of income earned from owning stocks, shares, and bonds—what is called rentier income—also rises as you move up the income ladder within the top 10 percent of income earners. While wages still made up a significant chunk of earnings (about 40 percent) for the top 0.01 percent of households in 2007, earnings from dabbling in capital markets are about a third on the earnings.[10] So to the growing inequality in compensation and wages add the concentration of stock and capital ownership in the hands of the wealthiest households.

More evidence of this highly skewed income distribution can be gleaned from the IRS report of the top 400 taxpayers in the US. The share of this select group rose from 46.6 million in 1992 to

173.9 million before the dot-com bust in 2000–01 to a whopping US$344.8 million in 2007. The share of wage income in the annual income of these taxpayers fell from 26 percent to 6.6 percent over this period even as the share of capital gains increased from 36 to 66 percent.[11]

This growing polarization of the economy reflected the restructuring of class relations after the coup of finance. Income was redistributed away from workers as wages were squeezed and an assault was launched on the working class. This process involved the defeat of working class aspirations and the smashing of unions.[12] The manner in which bailout of the auto maker Chrysler was affected under the Carter administration in1979 was a signal of this shift. In 1979, as the second oil shock pushed the debt-ridden Chrysler over edge toward bankruptcy, the federal government and the creditor banks put together a loan guarantee that forced the United Auto Workers Union to accept a wage freeze and cuts in benefits amounting to nearly US$500 million (followed in a year by further wage cuts) even as the new head Lee Iacocca proceeded to become in five years the highest paid US executive in the world.[13] The success of the banks in enforcing wage concessions paved the way for a reordering of class relations, the marginalization of unions, and the retreat of what has been called "big labor." This pattern of concessions to management (at the behest of the creditors) spread across industry. The decisive smashing of the Air Traffic Controllers strike in 1981, when Reagan brought in military air traffic controllers to replace the striking workers and announced the dismissal of the members of the relatively new union the Professional Air Traffic Controllers Organization that had organized the strike, was a defining moment in the assault on working class mobilization in the US.[14]

The growth in unemployment was the backdrop for launching this attack on union power. Union density has fallen from 30 percent of employed workers to about 12 percent. Unemployment nearly doubled from about 5 percent in 1979 when the aggressive attack on inflation was launched, to nearly 10 percent by 1982 (Figure 5.7).

The decade of the 1990s in the US is held up as the period of the Great Moderation—when the "goldilocks" economy was growing at a rate that was neither too hot nor too cold and both volatility and inflation were held in check. This period in fact witnessed the erosion of jobs in the manufacturing sector, particularly in those sectors that faced competition from cheap imports. In the toys, clothing, and electronic goods sectors, 40 percent of displaced persons were still out of work two years later or had suffered

Figure 5.7. Union Density (left hand axis) and the Growth of Unemployment (right hand axis)

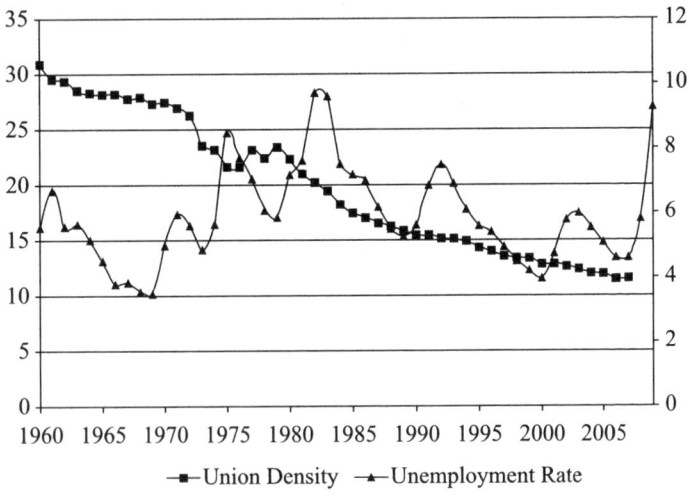

Source: OECD, Bureau of Labor Statistics.

wage cuts of at least 15 percent.[15] The jobs that were being created continued to be largely in the nontraded services sector—flipping burgers, working in supermarkets, cleaning, and janitorial work. The recovery of employment in the latter half of the 1980s was thus primarily in low paying, low skill, service sector jobs. The falling ratio of minimum to average wages in the US, which declined from about 41 percent in 1975 to less than 25 percent in 2007, reflects the marginalization of labor (Figure 5.8). This marginalization becomes even more sharply evident if we compare this downward slide with the significantly higher ratio (around 55 percent) in France.[16]

And yet, despite this debilitating growth in inequality and stagnant wages, the US has sustained its role as the engine of world demand. This was made possible by the same process of

Figure 5.8. Minimum Wage Relative to Average Wage of the Full-Time Employee

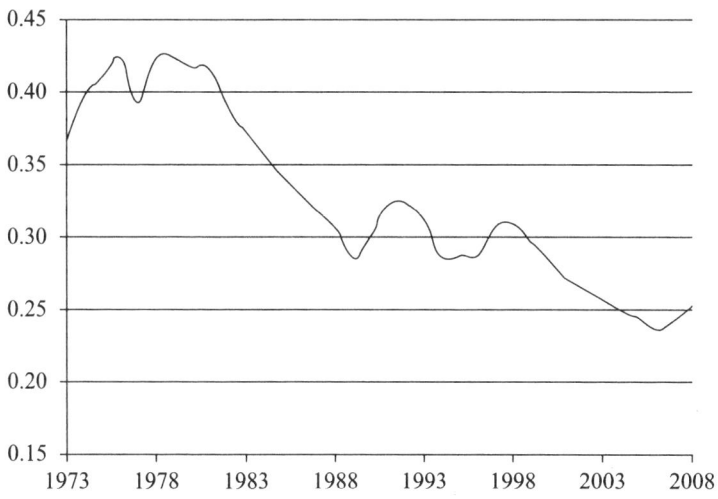

Source: OECD database.

financialization that had spurred financial sector profits. As the state retreated from the public provisioning of housing, health, and education services and retirement pensions, finance extended its tentacles more pervasively into working class households, offering credit cards, auto loans, student loans, mortgages pension schemes, and home equity loans. Thus the mandate for affordable housing during the Clinton period was pursued alongside the revamping of welfare that, in effect, drove a good chunk of the US poor out of the safety net of welfare. This process was given a further boost under the Bush administration.

The mass of workers and consumers have sunk deeper into debt, while finance has fattened on and penetrated more and more aspects of lives of ordinary people, sucking their earnings, and adding to the insecurity of their livelihoods.[17] This expropriation of worker incomes by finance also blunts the edge of worker resistance. A worker with an unpaid mortgage or a newly graduated student with thousands of dollars in loans is also less likely to organize against bad working conditions or the erosion of their incomes. The growing debt burden becomes a tool in the hands of financial and corporate capital to discipline the workforce.

Consumption demand has been growing as the savings rate has been squeezed. From an average about 10 percent of GDP in the 1970s, personal savings fell to an average rate of two percent between 1999 and 2004, briefly turning negative in 2005. Before the crisis, personal savings was at around one percent of GDP. The consumption binge has been stoked by the surge of consumer credit as the mass of employees and consumers have sunk deeper into debt.

The poorest households have a higher burden of debt both as a share of their income compared to all households. Since the 1990s, more than 25 percent of the households in the poorest fifth of the population owe more than 40 percent of their income in debt repayment. This share is double the share of all households (which was about 11 to 12 percent).[18] Credit card debt of an average American family increased by about 58 percent in the period between 1989 and 2004. About 67 percent of families with annual incomes less than US$10,000 (in US$2,000) had incurred credit card debt, and the debt of this group saw the largest increase, 342 percent compared to a 31 percent increase for families with incomes above US$100,000 between 1989 and 2004.[19] The financial burden of debt fell disproportionately on low-income working class families who are increasingly vulnerable to defaults. The imposition of harsher rules for personal bankruptcy in 2005 has meant that these households have little recourse to any relief.

As finance held sway over the economy, siphoning the earnings of workers and making rich returns through the plethora of new instruments and securities, it created an economy bloated by debt, and increasingly susceptible to the volatility of financial markets. This debt-fueled consumption demand is an extremely tenuous basis for growth and accumulation.[20]

GILDED AGE REDUX

The resurgence of finance ushered in a period that was in many ways reminiscent of the gilded age that preceded the Crash of 1929 and the Great Depression. In fact, if we take a longer view, the current levels of debt and the extraordinary prosperity at the top of the income ladder paralleled those witnessed during the gilded age of the 1920s. The share of the top 1 percent of households in income was around 23 percent at the peak before 1929, a level that was attained again only in 2006. The share of the top 0.1 percent of the households follows a similar U-shaped trajectory—rising to peak of near 12 percent in the 1920s, followed by a decade when the share fell, to begin rising again in the 1980s. By 2006, this share had crossed 12 percent (Figure 5.9).

A similar historical pattern is seen if we turn to the share of private debt (Figure 5.10). Private debt as a ratio to GDP rose through the 1920s, peaking at little less than two and half times US GDP in 1932.[21] Since then, the debt share declined sharply, picking up once again after the Second World War. The pace accelerated in the 1980s and 1990s, surging to a level that was three times US GDP.

Figure 5.9. Polarization of Income

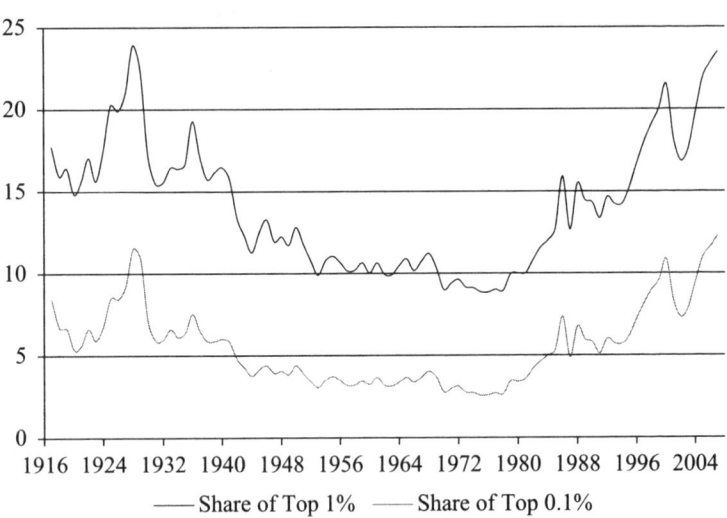

——— Share of Top 1%   ——— Share of Top 0.1%

Source: Piketty, T. and E. Saez. 2007. "Income and Wage Inequality in the US: 1913–2002" in A.B. Atkinson and T. Piketty (eds), *Top Incomes over the Twentieth Century*, Available at http://elsa.berkeley.edu/~saez/piketty-saezOUP04US.pdf.

Figure 5.10. Yoked to Debt (Private Debt as Ratio to GDP)

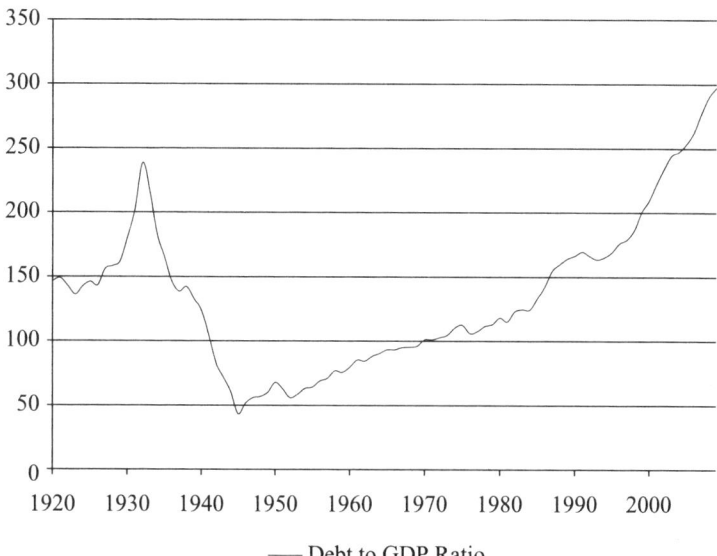

—— Debt to GDP Ratio

Source: Keen, S. 2009. "The Credit Tsunami." in G. Friedman, F. Moseley, and C. Sturr (eds), *The Economic Crisis Reader*, New York: Dollars and Sense.

A study of how banking salaries compared with those in other sectors brings out the pattern even more clearly.[22] Through the 1920s and the early 1930s, banking wages relative to the nonfarm private sector were sharply in excess of the benchmark relative wage that accounted for differences in skills, training, and education (Figure 5.11). This premium that bankers extracted as a reward for their speculative acumen was squeezed with the institution of a tighter regulatory framework in the wake of the bank failures of the 1930s. Since the 1990s, this premium has soared again. It would seem that bankers earn more as they steer the financial sector toward greater risk taking.

Figure 5.11. The Banking Wage Premium

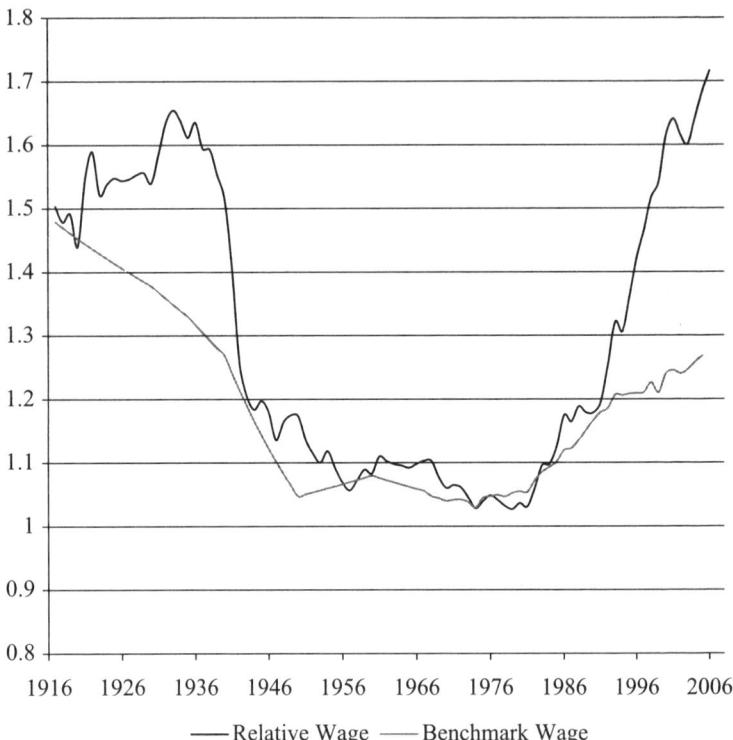

——— Relative Wage ——— Benchmark Wage

Source: Phillipon and Resheff. 2009. Wages and Human Capital in the US Banking Industry: 1909–2006. NBER Working Paper 14644.

The interwar years, before the Great Depression, were also years when finance and banking ruled the roost. The 1920s had seen a significant concentration of banking. Commercial banks forged deep links with the stock markets through their security affiliates. Large public corporations came to rely on the stock market for funding. Through the 1920s, the stock market promised seemingly endless gains, and banking was transformed from a staid stodgy profession to the exciting perilous world of breathless and cutthroat deal making, similar in many ways to the world of finance of the past two decades.

When the dizzying rise of stock markets in the 1920s came to an end with the Crash of 1929, banks that had provided the funds for this lending saw their asset base collapse. The rumors of vulnerable banks stoked a panic among the depositors whose savings had been entrusted to these banks. The bank runs and bank failures in the first years of the 1930s signaled the onset of the Great Depression and a massive squeeze of output and employment followed. Unemployment in these years rose to around 24 percent. The New Deal Programs to provide relief, foster recovery, and initiate reforms were launched as a response to this experience. It was, however, only after the massive spending on the War that output and employment revived.

The Great Depression and Second World War set in motion structural and legislative changes that sought to rein in the stranglehold of finance. The state took on the responsibility for regulating production and employment and providing social security and inserted itself into the process of engineering agreements in market sharing between corporations and wage setting between employers and unions. The postwar period was marked by an exceptional phase of rising wages, productivity, and profits in what has been christened the golden age of capitalism. Workers through rising wages and unionization had managed to share in the gains of the productivity boom of this period.

By the 1960s, however, the dynamic of the golden age began to run out of steam as a period of crisis and declining profitability began to slow down accumulation. The phenomena of stagflation—soaring inflation and growing unemployment—plagued the US economy. Rising wages and the demands of the working class came to be blamed for fueling this inflationary spiral and for squeezing profits. The role of state interventions and spending on welfare programs was also called into question and momentum gathered on initiatives to dismantle the regulatory structure that had attempted to tame finance.

These structural changes paved the way for a new gilded age under the hegemony of finance.[23] This new reign of finance has had important implications for the real economy, and for distribution and accumulation.

Neoliberalism and the Reign of Finance

As production in manufacturing has been rationalized by trimming the labor force, shifting to the employment of casual temporary labor, and through outsourcing of production, it has led to the polarization of incomes and the hollowing out of the middle class in the US. Since the launch of the neoliberal assault on workers, real wages of production workers have stagnated. During the "golden age" between 1948 and 1973, the annual rate of growth of average real income of the production worker had grown by 2.3 percent. In the neoliberal period, between 1979 and 2008, the growth of average real income slowed to a negligible 0.1 percent. In fact the decade between 1979 and 1990 witnessed a squeeze on real earnings, as incomes declined by 0.8 percent.[24] More importantly, wages have lagged behind productivity through most of the past four decades (Figure 5.12). Over the period 1979–2007, productivity (output per hour) rose by 1.91 percent. Average hourly earnings over this period were relatively stagnant, declining by about 0.04 percent.[25] After working faster and harder, workers are facing an erosion of earnings and are able to command only a declining share of the value of that they produce.

110

Figure 5.12. Workers' Earnings Lag Behind Productivity (Annual Growth Rates: Percentage)

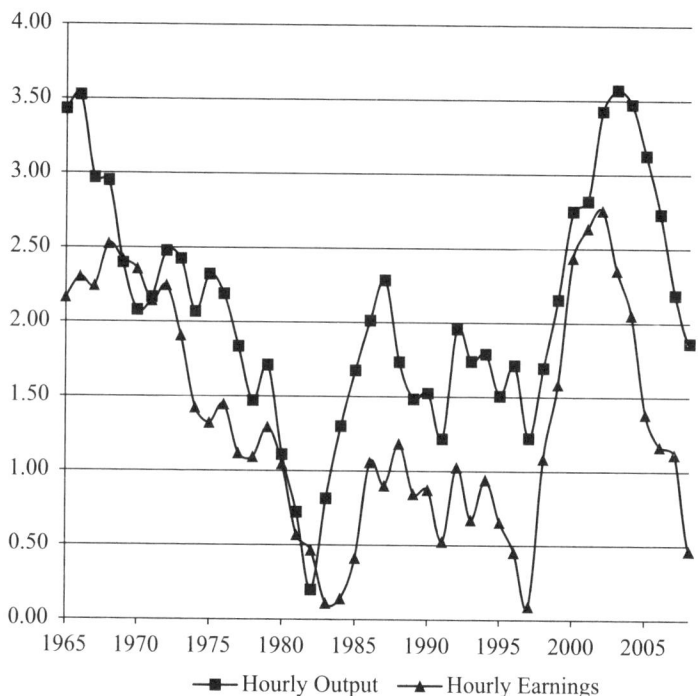

Source: Bureau of Labor Statistics.

As labor productivity outpaces real wages, the surplus created by the labor force—the difference between the value added by labor and the compensation paid to it—would swell. This is reflected in the restoration of profitability in the 1980s and 1990s (Figure 5.13). Without going into the vexed debate around how profit rates are calculated, a broad pattern can be discerned. After collapsing from its peak in the mid-1960s, the rate of profit showed signs of revival after the structural changes of the 1980s, even though it has not returned to its 1965 peak. Unlike the

Figure 5.13. Profit Rate (Corporate Nonfinancial Sector)

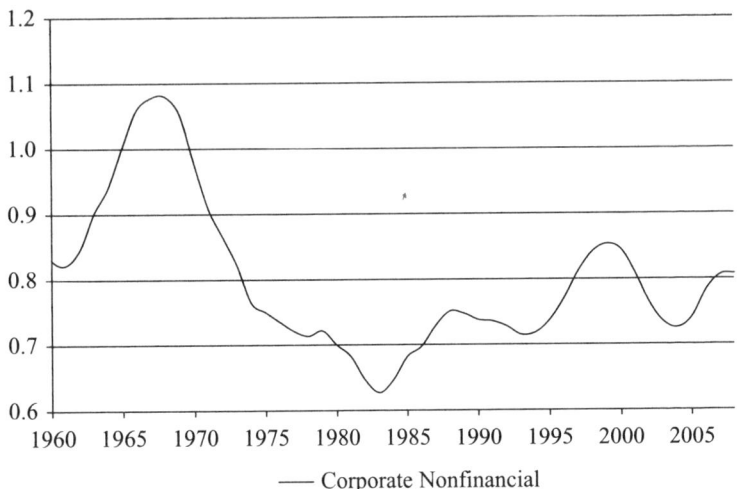

—— Corporate Nonfinancial

Source: Bureau of Economic Affairs.

stagflationary crisis of the 1970s that had been precipitated by the erosion of profitability, the structural underpinnings of the current crisis do not lie in a period of falling profitability.[26]

The source of the restoration of profitability can be discerned by looking at the trends in capital productivity (output–capital ratio) and the share of profit in total income (the profit share)—two components of the rate of profit (Figure 5.14). The profit rate declined through the 1970s, driven by a falling profit share and relatively stagnant capital productivity. Since the 1980s, the profit share has displayed a significant increase along with rising capital productivity, in particular through the 1990s, before capital productivity slumps sharply at the beginning of this decade. The revival of the profit rate in the 1990s was a direct outcome of capital's ability to squeeze the worker's share in income and extract greater increases in productivity.

Figure 5.14. Sources of Profitability

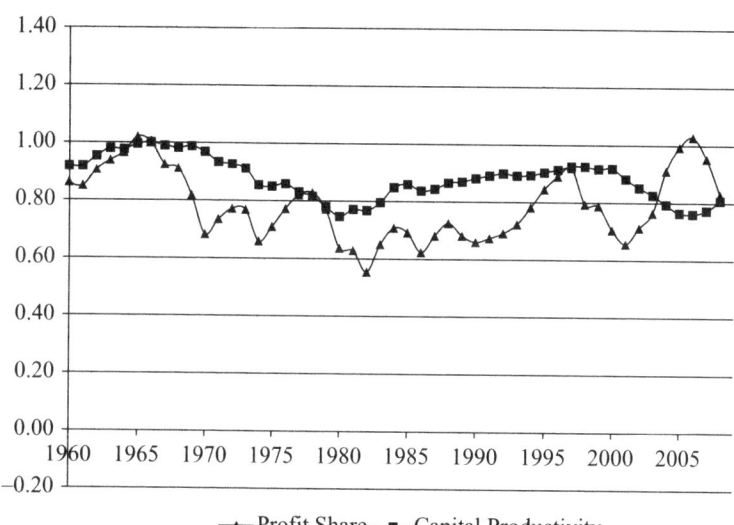

Source: Bureau of Economic Affairs.

These trends in productivity can be traced primarily to the whole-scale reorganization of work under the just-in-time systems. The contemporary workplace has been refashioned to speed up work, eliminate breaks and stoppages, promote flexible work groups that can be redeployed as needed by the manager and by imposing rigid systems of quality control that continually pressure workers to improve productivity by working harder and faster. This overhaul depended on an intensification of managerial control at the workplace to create what has been called the lean and mean workplace.[27] At the same time low-skilled manufacturing jobs have been relocated globally, leaving in place an extremely pared down workforce engaged in manufacturing.

An important dimension of these changes is not just the squeeze on workers, but also the concomitant rise of the importance of supervisory workers. The intensification of managerial control has also enhanced the role of the supervisory worker. The earnings of these supervisory workers have diverged significantly from those of ordinary production workers since the 1980s (Figure 5.15). Between 1948 and 1973, the average annual growth rate of earnings of production workers at 2.3 percent and supervisory workers at 2.1 percent moved fairly closely together. In the period after the Volcker shock, from 1979 to 2007, incomes of supervisory workers grow much more steeply at the rate of 2.1 percent per annum than the earnings of ordinary workers, which remained fairly stagnant (growing at around 0.1 percent per annum).[28]

A big chunk of rising profitability fostered by the neoliberal coup has thus been cornered by the rising executives and managerial class.[29]

Figure 5.15. Growth Rate of Incomes of Production Workers and Supervisory Workers

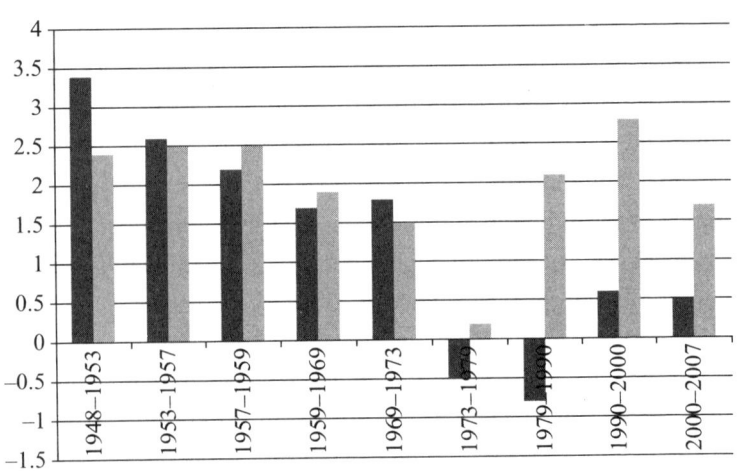

■ Production Worker   ■ Supervisory Worker

Source: Mohun, S. 2010. "The Crisis of 2008 in Historical Perspective," May, Table 4.

The rise and growing importance of this class, which was also evident in the economic polarization seen in the past two decades, is linked to the resurgence of finance.[30] The growth of finance is marked by the separation of ownership and control. The managerial class interposes itself between the shareholders and creditors and the worker.

Corporations are turning increasingly to capital markets to finance their investments. These investments increasingly take the form of leveraged buyouts that result in stripping and flipping the target company in the ruthless pursuit of greater efficiency while piling on the debt. The incentives for the manager, whose salaries and bonuses are linked to current performance and the gyrations of stock markets, get skewed toward chasing short-term returns and are marked by a growing distaste for tying up capital in illiquid long-term investments. The Enron and WorldCom debacles are testimony to these perverse incentives. These perverse incentives are also evident in the manner in which private equity groups plunged into the profitable business of buying up firms with borrowed funds. The buyout involved the groups paying out substantial fees to themselves, while piling on debt to the acquired company, and then flipping it over at a huge profit to another fund. At this stage, the firm got more encumbered with debt, workers were laid off, and benefits steadily pruned.

Finance appears to be increasingly autonomous of the real world—the sweat and grime of the factory—and increasingly dazzled by prospects of quick speculative profits. As profits are siphoned off into executive pay packages and financial dealings, real investment suffers and the pace of accumulation slows down. The rate of investment after mild upturn in the 1990s has slumped in the past decade. Even if we look at fixed nonresidential investment, the recovery of investment after 2002 was much less pronounced than that of the previous decade (Figure 5.16).

Figure 5.16. Rate of Investment (Percentage Share of GDP)

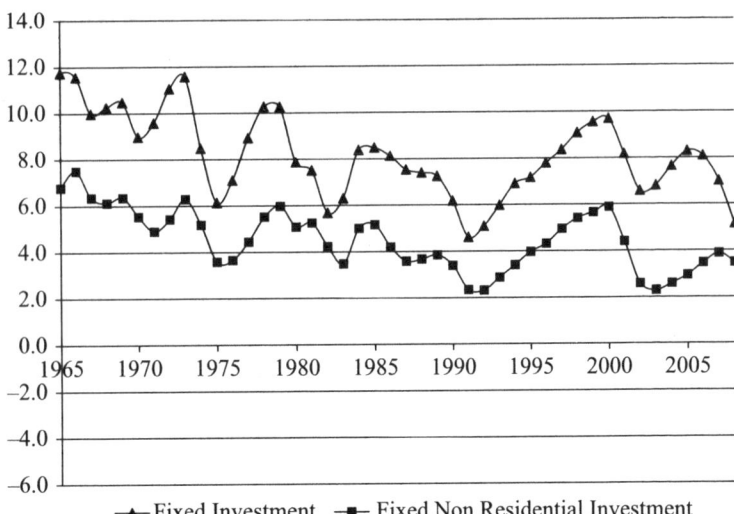

—▲— Fixed Investment   —■— Fixed Non Residential Investment

Source: Bureau of Economic Affairs, National Income and Production Accounts.

This slowdown in pace of accumulation is derived not so much from the disappearance of avenues of profitable and productive investment opportunities, but more fundamentally from the logic of financial dominance. Once again, the parallel to the Great Depression is striking.

POISED FOR A LONG SLUMP

The gilded age in the run up to the Great Depression was marked by favorable trends in profitability and productivity.[31] The rise of large public corporations gave a boost not just to the stock market frenzy of the 1920s but also to a significant managerial class, both in finance and in industry. The rise of finance and the managerial

116

elite in the early twentieth century wrought a sea change in the organization of industry and work, while forging a deep dependence on the burgeoning stock market with its close links to the commercial banking sector. This managerial and financial revolution emerged as a response and outcome to the structural crisis of the end of the nineteenth century when accumulation and profitability had eroded sharply. These structural changes paved the way for the gilded age, but also led to the crisis of the interwar years.

The aftermath of this crisis saw the rise of working class struggles and the power and wealth of finance and the managerial elite was relatively constrained. Keynes had famously exhorted for the euthanasia of the rentier, but even though the regulatory overhaul of the period clipped the wings of speculators, the rentier was far from being euthanized. Finance is integral to capitalist accumulation and while it did not enjoy the same hegemony it had held in the run up to the Great Depression, it remained a strong force, shaping for instance the Federal Reserve–Treasury accord of 1951 which insulated monetary policy from governmental control and established the basis for the deployment of anti-inflationary policy against workers' interests in the 1980s.[32]

The cracks in "Keynesian compromise" of the postwar world were exposed—as profitability and accumulation slowed in the 1960s, finance seized the initiative once again. The rising financial and managerial executive class helped engineer a transformation of work organization that fueled the growth in productivity. Financial innovations and the global integration of financial markets facilitated greater mobility of capital and further strengthened capital's ability to discipline the working class.

The current crisis is not just a crisis of this neoliberal model of capitalist accumulation that finance has imposed. It is more than that. It reflects the long-term structural patterns governing capitalist dynamics, its unstable contradictory character. Drawing on lessons of history to highlight the underlying structural dynamics behind the crisis should not, however, obscure the specific institutional context of the current crisis, but they do caution against a sanguine faith that a recovery can take place without dramatic structural changes. The outcome depends on how the balance of class forces is restructured in the current conjecture. Specifically, it depends on whether the power of finance can be contained. The policy response so far has not taken on this challenge headlong.

There is, however, another dimension to this crisis. The resurgence of finance is entwined with the ascent of the US to the position of a dominant imperial power and the emerging role of the dollar at the fulcrum of international flows of capital in the postwar global economy. The US in the interwar period was an emerging industrial power, not yet ready to challenge the global supremacy of England. Its currency was tied to gold and, unlike today, the country was a net saver and creditor. In fact, Britain had between 1925 and 1928 pushed the US to relax its monetary policy to facilitate the return to the gold standard, a factor often cited in explaining the stock market crash of 1929. However, when Britain went off the gold standard in 1931, the flight of gold from the US market exacerbated the crisis as the specter of the flight of gold hamstrung state efforts to pump the economy.

In contrast, the US, in the wake of the current crisis, has been pumping liquidity on an unprecedented scale, flooding the market with US treasury bills. To sustain the demand for US treasury bills, it is necessary for the US to protect its status as the desired global safe-haven currency. This status hinges on the privileged role of the dollar in international financial markets. The crisis cannot be fully explained without comprehending the global dominance of the dollar as a key currency.

Chapter 6

Dollar Rules

The current crisis is not only the bust that follows the housing boom.…
It's basically the end of a 60-year period of continuing credit expansion
based on the dollar as the reserve currency.

— George Soros at the World Economic Forum at Davos, January 2008

When the US subprime markets began to unravel in the summer of 2007, the impact was felt in financial markets across the Atlantic. The securitization of loans had helped further the hegemony of finance globally by creating financial products that were bought and sold globally. Now these same investors began pulling out of esoteric financial products. Commodity exporters thrived on the basis of the boom in prices as the unwinding of the shadow banking system sent investors scrambling for returns to the commodity futures market. Emerging markets, for a period, saw an increase in investment flows. Even as capital flowed out of the US in the wake of the unraveling shadow banking system, capital flows to emerging markets continued to rise and flows to developing countries surged in 2007 by about 40 percent from its 2006 level.[1] The dollar faced a widespread sell off. After five years of decline in which it had lost about 25 percent of its value against a basket of currencies, the dollar plunged sharply to an unprecedented low of around US$1.48 against the euro in January 2008, a fall of about 40 percent from its 2002 peak. It seemed as if the fate of the dollar hung in the balance.

DOLLAR HEGEMONY

Paradoxically, the complete seizure of credit and finance after the collapse of Lehman and the specter of a systemic crisis on the scale of the Great Depression heralded a turnaround for the dollar. The crisis of confidence that seized the financial markets led to a flight to "safety." At a time when markets did not have any confidence in the ability of debtors to honor their debts and froze lending, US treasury bills appeared the safest bet. For any other country, the systemic failure of the domestic financial sector would have precipitated capital flight and a currency crisis. In fact, the previous three decades are littered with episodes of currency crisis triggered by capital flight in response to collapsing financial markets—Brazil and Argentina in 1994, Thailand and Korea in 1997, Russia in 1998, and Turkey in 2002, to name a few. In contrast, the sale of dollars that had continued through August 2008 came to a halt with the bankruptcy of Lehman.

The explanation of this paradox lies in the privileged position of the dollar globally as the dominant key currency. As a key currency the dollar is the main currency used both to denominate and settle international transactions. The dollar is the unit of account for the bulk of trade and financial flows. In 2007, as the subprime market burst, the dollar entered on one side of 86 percent of all foreign exchange transactions, while its closest competitor, the euro, entered on one side of 37 percent of foreign exchange transactions. Since debt and international payment obligations are settled largely in terms of dollars, countries also hold a significant share of their reserves as dollars. About 66 percent of foreign exchange reserves are held in dollars, while the euro share of foreign exchange reserves is about 25 percent.[2]

The fact that the rest of the globe uses dollars for its international dealings places the US in a unique position. The external debt and deficits of the US can be financed by issuing IOUs in the form of dollars and US treasury bills. In that sense the US enjoys an elastic credit line that is not available to most other countries. The difference is that US debt is in its own currency. Its deficits flood the rest of the world with dollar liquidity. And so the US enjoys what has been called an "exorbitant privilege."

When the crisis gripped the global economy, investors all over the world chose to put their money in US treasury bills and stockpile dollar reserves. Financial institutions hoarded cash and demanded ever-widening premiums before lending to one another. The commercial paper market that serves as a source of short-term funding for the corporate sector dried up. The central bank was the only institution willing to lend, and the debt of the US government appeared the safest investment in the wake of the financial implosion.

This sudden insatiable thirst for dollars in overseas centers such as London and Frankfurt propelled the currency higher. The dollar began to rise against a host of currencies (excluding the yen) as US investors repatriated funds and speculators turned increasingly averse to risk, launching a fire sale of a wide-range higher yielding assets (deleveraging) amid the growing turmoil. Even as the credit machinery remained jammed and the US Treasury and the Fed was floundering through the different incarnations of the TARP plan, the global demand for treasury bills kept growing. The Fed addressed the dollar drought by extending massive swap lines with overseas central banks and prepared to pour about US$630 billion into global markets to ease international money markets in October 2008.

The credit crisis has brought the role of the dollar as international money into stark relief. There is, however, nothing preordained or immutable about the dollar's privileged role. Before the First World War, from about the last quarter of the nineteenth century, the world operated on what was called the International Gold Standard when the British sterling was the dominant key currency. Prior to that, bullion was used to settle international payments. The dollar's role as internationally accepted money is the outcome of the historical evolution of the US as the financial center of the global economy and as the dominant imperialist power.

The dollar has now survived more than two decades of growing US deficits and debts and two cycles of appreciation and depreciation (Figure 6.1). The global appetite for dollars that allowed the US an easy access to global savings has been sustained by the privileged role of the dollar as international money. The US's ability to attract willing holders of its public debt in the form of holdings of reserves and treasury bills depended not just on the central position of the US in international financial markets but also on ensuring international support through the assertion of imperial power, whether through strategic alliances, diplomatic negotiations, or military threat. The dominance of finance and the central position of US financial markets in the pyramid of global capital markets have helped preserve the privileged position of the dollar and the structural vulnerability of the periphery. This includes both surplus countries (that are not competing with the dollar as international money like China and Japan) whose export-led growth strategy ties their economies closely to the US appetite for imports and the debtor countries of the periphery (Latin America and South East Asia), which have borne the brunt of deflationary pressures and fragility.[3]

122

Figure 6.1. US Current Account Deficit and the Movement of the Dollar

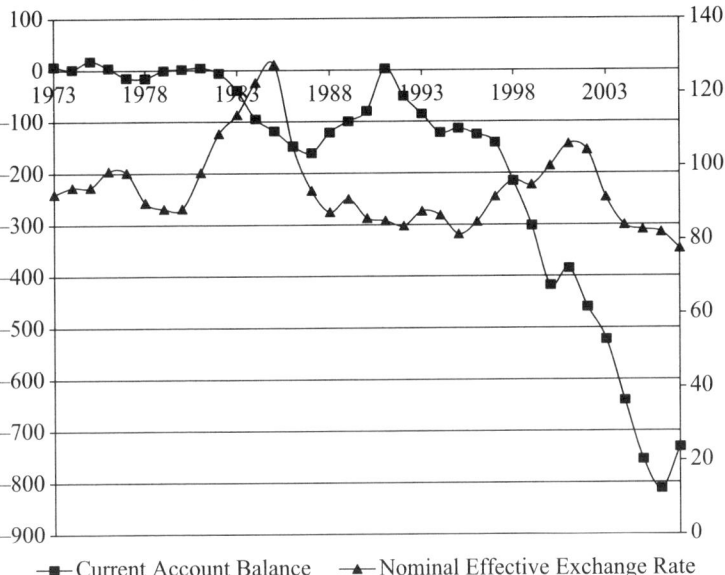

—■—Current Account Balance   —▲—Nominal Effective Exchange Rate

Source: Bureau of Economic Affairs, International Financial Statistics.

Note: The right axis shows the nominal effective exchange rate of the dollar (trade weighted index of average value of currency) with the rate in 2000 set at 100. The left hand axis shows the US current account balance in US$ billion.

To comprehend the resilience of the dollar's role as the dominant international money, we need to explore how this dollar standard was established after the Second World War in the Bretton Woods system, and how the role of the dollar was extended once this system collapsed. The mechanisms that sustained the privileged role of the dollar are linked to the dominance of the neoliberal ideology and finance, and more particularly to the particular manner in which the US exercised its imperial power in this period.

123

ESTABLISHING THE DOLLAR STANDARD

In the aftermath of the Second World War, Britain's imperial position was greatly weakened, and it was facing significant balance of payments pressures. The US emerged as the largest creditor country, with substantial foreign exchange reserves. However, in order for the dollar to play the role of the dominant currency, there had to be enough dollars to go around. The critical problem of the dollar shortage—finding means by which war-ravaged Europe could finance its dependence on US imports for reconstruction—needed to be solved. Britain, with its deep and liquid financial markets was integral to the US project of rebuilding the multilateral trading system. At the same time the establishment of the dollar as an international currency involved preempting the resurgence of the pound sterling after the war. The intense negotiations during the Bretton Woods Conference reflected the tensions and contradictions of reshaping the international monetary system under the hegemony of the dollar.[4] The outcome of the discussions around the rival plans of John Maynard Keynes who headed the British delegation and Harry Dexter White who led the American delegation was in effect to cement the role of the dollar. Under the Bretton Woods system, the dollar was pegged to gold (at US$35/ounce of gold), while all other currencies were pegged to the dollar.

The International Monetary Fund (IMF) created as a result of the Bretton Woods conference was initially conceived of as an instrument to facilitate expansionary national economic policies, enabling member countries to overcome temporary liquidity problems, such as a shortage of loan funds and balance of payment crisis. However, the IMF played only a small role in the postwar reconstruction, in large part due to US efforts to marginalize its role in the emerging world order by imposing stringent conditions on countries that sought to draw funds from the IMF. Instead, the offsetting capital flows needed to facilitate the financing of balance of payments deficits of Europe and Japan were provided under the US initiatives for postwar reconstruction plans—the Marshall and Dodge plans. The imperative of ensuring that Europe did not evolve into a monetary area insulated from the dollar area by permanent controls remained a pressing concern.[5] The outbreak of the Korean War and the domestic thrust toward rearmament within the US formed the context for a transformation of the character of loan assistance to that of military aid. Military aid provided Europe with the means of financing imports from the US after the Marshall plan had lapsed. These postwar reconstruction plans along with economic and military aid by the US helped to buttress the role of the dollar.

The Suez Crisis in 1956 (the military confrontation launched by Britain, France, and Israel when after Nasser announced the nationalization of the Suez Canal) was an important milestone in the forging of the dollar standard. It signaled the effective eclipse of the pound's role as international money and also marked a shift in Washington's attitude to the IMF. The IMF was drafted into the rescue of the pound from speculative attacks that threatened to deplete Britain's dollar reserves in the aftermath of the attack on Egypt was launched.[6] The US was able to use the promise of an IMF bailout to affect the ouster of Britain from the Suez, while minimizing its own direct financial contribution to Britain's rescue. The reinstatement of capital controls following this crisis restricted the use of the pound by British banks to finance trade between countries outside the sterling area. British financiers began to resort to offering dollar loans against their dollar deposits, drawing Britain more closely into the ambit of American imperial power.[7] Thus the role of London as a financial center was preserved, while cementing its ties to the international hegemony of the dollar.

The European Payments Union had been formed in 1950 to ease the settlement problems posed by the dollar shortage in Europe. With the dissolution of the Union and the restoration of currency convertibility (on current account) in Europe in 1958, the US attempt to forge an international monetary order pegged on the dollar was brought to fruition. However, as Europe and Japan emerged as industrial competitors of the US, its current account balances began deteriorating through the 1960s. The possibility of a speculative run on the US gold stock (as the nations holding dollars began to demand gold in exchange for them) posed a threat to the international payments mechanism. France and Germany both grew uneasy with the dollar's "exorbitant privilege" as the anchor of the Bretton Woods system. The period was rife with talk and prognostications of a dollar crisis. The sterling devaluation in 1967 (followed by the franc in 1969), the upward speculative pressure on gold prices, and the escalating costs of financing the war in Vietnam brought the Crisis to a head.

At the heart of this crisis was the contradiction of the role of the dollar as international money. The dwindling gold stocks and the emerging deficits of the US reflected the cost of being the banker to the world. If the world was to have enough dollars to finance international flows, the US needed to sustain a deficit and debt. The problem arose because the growing debt burden necessary to fuel international liquidity could erode confidence in the dollar. This is the crux of the dilemma posed by the use of a country's currency as international money.

In 1971, Nixon unilaterally announced that the US would no longer be exchanging gold for dollar liabilities. The closing of the gold window and the "floating" of the dollar in 1973 did not result in the displacement of the dollar as the international reserve currency.[8] Instead, developments in international monetary arrangements over the next three decades enabled the preservation of the role of the dollar as international money in the form of the floating dollar standard. At the heart of this process was the emergence and rapid growth of unregulated international financial flows.

The aggressive advocacy of liberalization of financial markets and the dismantling of capital controls were pursued as a way to encourage private international capital flows denominated in dollars. Dominance in the global financial markets came to underpin the role of its currency as international money. At the same time dollar hegemony and the central role of the US in international financial markets would be crucial to the growing economic and political dominance of finance globally. There is an inherent logic in the evolution of the growing external deficits for the imperial power that plays the role of the banker to the world. It depends upon and fosters the rise to dominance of finance.

US bankers were strong advocates of moves to liberalize and deregulate finance. Thus, the strong opposition from New York bankers to the provisions for capital controls (which could limit the movement of dollars around the world) in the Bretton Woods agreement stemmed from their fears of the erosion of the profitable business of receiving money fleeing Europe, and, more importantly, the possibility that London could use exchange controls to preempt the ascendancy of the dollar in the international monetary system.

The Eurodollar market, comprising of dollar-denominated bank deposit liabilities held in foreign banks or in foreign branches of US banks received an impetus after the UK hiked interest rates and restrictive capital controls in the aftermath of the Suez Crisis.

This market arose as a consequence of British banks substituting an international financial business based in sterling for one based in dollars as a way of preserving the role of the city of London in the face of the erosion of the sterling's importance as an international reserve.[9] With the capital controls instituted by the US after 1964 to curb the speculative flight from the dollar, US banks began to finance their operations through the Eurodollar markets as a way of evading restrictive capital controls. For the big players in the financial hubs of London and New York, these markets emerged as a means of capturing profits while bypassing regulatory controls. The Eurodollar market grew in the face of growing efforts in the US to prevent capital flight expanding from US$9 billion in 1964 to US$145 billion 1971.[10] The massive growth of this offshore market signaled the decisive shift away from the restrictive Bretton Woods system with a greater focus on the advocacy of financial openness and integration in the interests of preserving dollar dominance.

With the collapse of the Bretton Woods arrangements, this unregulated market came to be the anchor of the international monetary system.[11] The move in favor of liberalized capital flows signaled by the elimination of capital controls in the US in 1974 gave a further boost to this market. With Germany and France showing increasing reluctance to fund US deficits in the context of growing inflationary pressures, the US turned to the accumulating surpluses of the OPEC countries after the cartel raised prices precipitating the oil shock of 1973. The US government agenda at this juncture was to ensure that these surpluses were recycled through international financial markets, primarily Eurodollar markets, so that the funds were routed through American banks. US political and economic power ensured that these surpluses were recycled through the private channels of the

Eurodollar markets.[12] As the dollar denominated surpluses of the OPEC countries came to be recycled through this market in the 1970s, the market grew to be a full-fledged capital market expanding to US$1.4 trillion in 1981—10 times its size in 1971.[13] This growing offshore market, which was both liquid and unregulated, proved an important means for encouraging foreign investors to finance the US deficit.

EXPORTING CRISIS TO THE PERIPHERY

Even as the regulation of financial markets in the US was being dismantled, a concerted campaign was launched to liberate economies in Latin America from the yoke of "financial repression." Disinflation, deregulation, and the freeing of the interest rates in these countries fueled a wave of inflows of private foreign capital. The oil surpluses that were absorbed into US money center banks like Citibank (which lent not simply to consumers but to governments, corporations, and other banks) through the Eurodollar markets were channeled to the emerging markets, in particular in Latin America, through syndicated loans, through the 1970s. These syndicated loans involved two or more banks jointly agreeing to make a loan to a sovereign borrower at a variable interest rate. Syndication allowed smaller financial institutions to acquire emerging market exposure under the "leadership" of larger banks that organized the syndicate, without actually having to establish a local presence. Syndicated lending to emerging market borrowers grew from small amounts in the early 1970s to US$46 billion in 1982, steadily displacing bilateral lending.[14] These government-guaranteed loans were actively promoted, both as being low risk and offering higher returns from that on

US bonds. While encouraging this flurry of investment in Latin American loans, the Citibank Chief Walter Wriston is supposed to have famously noted, "Governments don't go bankrupt."

The debt of these developing countries doubled from 8 percent of GDP in the beginning of the 1970s to about 22 percent of GDP in 1982. Mexico, Brazil, Venezuela, and Argentina together accounted for nearly 75 percent of total third world debt in this period. At the same time the dollar composition of the debt of developing countries grew from 47 percent to more than 60 percent in 1982.[15]

The 1979 hike of interest rates by Federal Reserve chairman Paul Volcker led to the steep increase in debt repayment commitments for emerging countries, precipitating the debt crisis of the 1980s. Like the recipients of the pernicious adjustable rate mortgages, sovereign borrowers who had gorged on the bonanza of cheap credit in the 1970s were now faced with interest rates that had spiked up sharply. In August 1982, Mexico suspended interest payments on its sovereign debt. Other countries including Brazil, Argentina, Venezuela, and the Philippines soon followed it. Lending came to an abrupt halt as the debt crisis exploded, posing a severe threat to the health of the big banks. American banks and financial institutions were severely overextended in Latin America and the syndication of loans implied a concentration of risks. Of the sovereign debt, 80 percent was concentrated among nine money center banks. The urgency for bail out efforts was a consequence of the need to secure the financial system from the repercussions of the debt defaults. The initial policy solution was to reschedule existing debt, arrange new lending, and require that the developing economy governments implement austere fiscal and monetary policies that would facilitate the eventual repayment of the still growing debt burden.

With the coup of finance, the neoliberal model was also pushed globally as a means of sustaining the dollar's international role, in particular, by sucking developing country markets into the orbit of finance. It marked an important juncture in US imperial relations, bringing countries of the periphery deeper into the embrace of the dollar empire. The debt crisis became the means by which a further impetus was given to liberalization of financial markets in emerging markets. The structural adjustment and stabilization programs imposed through the ages of the IMF and the World Bank were pivotal in furthering this transformation. The Bretton Woods institutions were refashioned under the so-called "Washington Consensus" into a means of imposing deflationary policies of fiscal austerity and monetary stringency on indebted developing countries. The debt conditionality associated with the bailout loan packages of the IMF enforced a policy shift to deregulating financial markets and promoting international capital flows.

Following Brazil's declaration of a moratorium on medium- and long-term payments in 1987, Citibank wrote down a large proportion of its emerging market loans transferring US$3 billion to a special reserve fund against possible loan losses in its developing country portfolio. Several large US banks followed suit. These special reserve funds were deployed as buffers and served to grant a greater degree of flexibility and bargaining power to the creditor banks. The aim was to ensure a resolution through voluntary debt reduction rather than debt forgiveness. These moves catalyzed the negotiation of a plan initiated by US Treasury Secretary Nicholas Brady—the Brady Plan—in 1989. The plan was based on a market-oriented approach that pushed the liberalization of financial markets in Latin America. The key element of the Brady Plan for dealing with the debt crisis was the transformation of debt to equity in the form of tradable bonds. The sale of these bonds would allow creditors to diversify sovereign risk more widely across international capital markets. At the same time emerging market countries would become more dependent on these international capital markets for their financing needs.

A Brady bond is essentially a structured product like the mortgage-backed securities. The developing country uses foreign exchange reserves to create an investment company. The investment company then uses its equity to buy long-term US Treasury bonds to serve as collateral against which it can issue its own fixed-interest liabilities—the Brady bonds. These bonds were proposed as a means of diversifying sovereign risk away from commercial banks and more widely across international capital markets. Banks switched from the syndicated sovereign loans to "Brady bonds," which could be traded at values determined by changes in the country's sovereign credit rating and in US interest rates. US institutional investors were limited to investments in assets with a minimum of risk (an "investment grade" credit rating). This meant that a large proportion of institutional investment funds were prevented from investing in emerging markets. Structured derivative packages, created by global investment banks, provided the means to circumvent these restrictions. Investment banks began to extend the Brady principle to other types of developing country debt, creating structured loans.[16] Lending through the capital markets was extended to private enterprises.

Private capital flows to emerging markets revived in the 1990s. Apart from Latin America, South East, and East Asia become important recipients of private capital flows in the 1990s. Foreign direct investment and portfolio investments now came to play a greater role in resource transfers to emerging markets. Offshore SPVs were sponsored and then used to transfer debt off the books. A Korean bank could set up such a vehicle under the tutelage of an American investment bank and then use this entity to borrow short-term paper using assets transferred by the parent bank to the shell company. This method was also attractive to US banks keen on gaining access to the Korean market since it allowed them to get around governmental controls that prevented foreign investors from owning more than 20 percent of the market.[17]

The surge in lending to developing countries in the 1990s was also characterized by the increased use of over-the-counter derivatives contracts as the vehicle for lending. The average daily turnover in foreign exchange markets grew from US$820 billion in 1992 to US$1.9 trillion in 2004 and was around US$3.2 trillion in 2007. In the same period, the average daily turnover of nontraditional foreign exchange transactions (over-the-counter derivatives) grew from US$1.2 trillion in 1992 to US$ 2.4 trillion in 2004, to reach US$4.2 trillion in 2007.[18] The switch to floating exchange rates created a huge demand for innovative means of managing the risks of global investment. Derivatives trade proliferated in the context of the volatility created by floating exchange rates and unregulated capital flows. Investors began to trade aggressively in derivatives in order to hedge against swings in exchange rates and interest rates or against the possibility of default investors in foreign markets.

Derivatives are pure pricing contracts that bet on the movement of underlying assets. The future's option for instance allows the investor to lock in a specified price at which to sell or buy a currency in the future. The investor can choose depending on how the market plays, whether or not to exercise the option to buy or sell a currency in the future. A swap entails an investor undertaking a contract to buy a currency at a specified price today and sell the currency back at a specified price at a future date. Similar derivative contracts could be executed to hedge against the movements in interest rates. But, as was seen in the context of the evolution of complex structured products like CDOs, these derivatives became a means of exploiting the potential profits of interest rate and exchange rate movements while expanding leverage.

A derivative contract that became extremely popular in South East Asia was the Total Return Swaps. An interest rate swap is a contract where an investor agrees to pay a fixed interest for a specified period in return for variable interest payments. An investor in South East Asia borrowing dollars at the standard lending rate and then using these funds to invest in a higher yielding short-term asset domestically ran the risk of a currency mismatch—it was borrowing in dollars and lending, in say, the local currency. Regulators generally discourage such a mismatch because of the exchange rate risk involved. A sudden devaluation of the baht would wipe out any profits. The Total Return Swap allowed the player to capture the potential profit of borrowing a low interest rate currency and lending in a higher interest rate currency without incurring regulatory surcharges or sanctions! So a Thai bank could borrow the dollars at the regular rate from the money center bank while paying out the interest and in capital gains baht on the Thai asset, without any debt in its books. The swap could also be used as way for the American or European money center bank to lend to a Thai bank without having to set aside capital according to the Basle requirements while earning a fat commission income. The Total Return Swap could also be used by an International money center bank to swap the return on higher risk Indonesian corporate bonds for the return on a loan to a Korean bank. In the event of a failure of the Indonesian corporation, the Korean bank would have to shell out the default amount to the international bank. This meant that a collapse in Indonesia could potentially lead to Korean banks becoming insolvent, so that there would be a contagion effect of these interconnected contracts.[19]

These derivative contracts and structured products were supposed to facilitate international capital flows by unbundling risk and redistributing it toward investors who were more willing and able to bear the exposure. They were individually tailored under the sponsorship of US and European banks and negotiated over-the-counter outside any kind of regulated exchange. Derivative trade became an effective means of evading regulatory control and tax laws. The creative accounting fostered in guise of exotic products promoted more opaque and more highly leveraged financial structures engendering greater fragility. The collapse of these markets was an important trigger for the Asian financial crises in 1997. Once again, the crisis was used as a mechanism for strengthening the grip of finance on these countries by enforcing further restructuring financial and industrial institutions through even more stringent loan conditionalities.[20]

The agenda of financial liberalization aggressively pursued through the IMF rescue packages in the 1980s and 1990s subjected emerging markets to the dominance of US finance and dollar hegemony. In 1990, dollars accounted for only 45 percent of reserves and deposits. Boosted by burgeoning private capital inflows into developing country markets and the growth of reserve holdings through the 1990s, the US dollar's share rose by 1998 to about 70 percent of holdings, a level not seen since the 1970s. In the same period, the dollar composition of long-term debt increased from about 46 percent to over 64 percent.

DOLLAR AND THE DOMINANCE OF FINANCE

The international system came to be remolded as a floating dollar standard after the collapse of the Bretton Woods system and private capital flows to developing countries were fostered as a means of entrenching these regions more deeply within the embrace of US hegemony and the sway of the dollar. Private capital flooded developing country markets in three broad waves. The first wave was marked by the aggressive pursuit of sovereign debt by US money center banks until the debt crisis of the 1980s brought this bonanza of cheap loans to an end. Capital flows received renewed impetus in the 1990s with the liberalization of financial markets in the periphery and the proliferation of global financial instruments and securities through the 1990s. This second wave came to an abrupt halt with the Asian Crisis of 1998. Most recently, since 2002 there has been a fresh surge of inflows to emerging markets, with private capital inflows rising from US$152 billion in 2002 to more than US$560 billion at the end of 2006.

Private capital flows after 1973 display an interesting pattern (Figure 6.2). As periods of inflows to emerging markets come to a halt in the wake of the Crisis, a surge of inflows to the US occurs. The resumption of private flows to emerging markets, on the other hand, signals a fresh outflow of capital from the US. This pattern of flows, where private investment flows were drawn into the US in a cyclical manner following the collapse of a surge of capital to emerging markets in the periphery, helped preserve the international role of the dollar.[21] Fostered by the growing dominance of finance, these waves of private capital flows to emerging markets have acted as a safety valve mechanism that has allowed the generation of international liquidity along with the growing US deficits without precipitating a speculative attack on the dollar.[22]

Through most of this period, under the floating dollar standard, the brunt of financial fragility was borne disproportionately by countries in the periphery. Between 1973 and 1997, 44 episodes of financial crises were witnessed in the advanced capitalist core

Figure 6.2. Net Private Capital Flows (US$ Million)

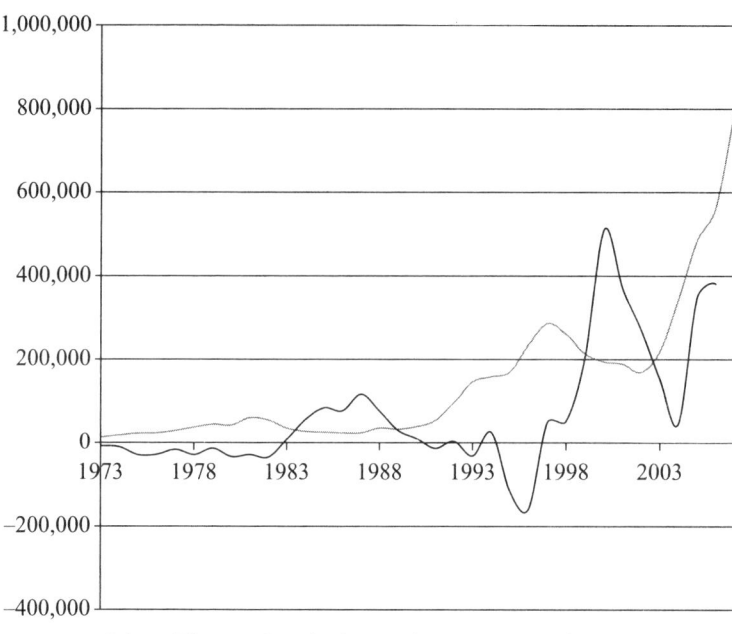

—— Private Flows to Developing Markets —— Net Private Flows to US

Source: Bureau of Economic Affairs, Global Development Finance.

countries and 95 in the periphery.[23] If one compares this to the period between 1945 and 1971 when there were 38 crises, it does seem as if the age of financialization was also an age of the Crisis.[24] In a sense, the Crisis in the periphery acted like a safety valve for the international monetary system hinged on dollar liquidity. Capital flight into dollars in the aftermath of the Crisis preserved the role of the dollar. At the same time the responses to the Crisis—the bailout packages—were geared to reinforcing the dominance of finance centered in the US.

Financial integration imparted a greater elasticity to the adjustment mechanisms in the core, and the proliferation of financial

137

instruments, and the surge of financial flows played an important role in preserving and extending the role of the dollar as world currency. The pivotal role of the US in global financial markets has reinforced the privileged status of the dollar enabling the US to generate international liquidity by running up its trade deficits and external debt. Apart from private investors official investors and central banks too became embroiled in the preservation of the role of the dollar. The Plaza Accord in 1985 committed the other advanced capitalist countries (Japan, Germany, France, and the UK) to adjust their monetary and fiscal policies in order to effect an orderly depreciation of the dollar. Foreign central banks undertook interventions in defense of the dollar and official purchases of dollars received the first big boost since the collapse of the Bretton Woods arrangements. This set the stage for what has been called a "Revived Bretton Woods" arrangement with the central bank holding of reserves of US treasury bills playing an important part in the multilateral clearing mechanisms of the floating dollar regime.[25] This is the other prong of the US ability to preserve the dominance of the dollar. The official demand for US treasury bills serves as the basis for the profusion of private financial flows.

Japan was the principal creditor country through the 1990s with the largest holdings of US reserves. The 1985 Plaza Accord, which started the deep and long appreciation of the yen, also set the stage for the decade-long stagnation in Japan. The 1995 "Reverse Plaza Accord," which engineered an appreciation of the dollar in relation to the yen ostensibly to stop a collapse of the Japanese economy, was more significantly a response to finance capital's push for a strong dollar policy. This helped precipitate the Asian economic crisis because the exports of many Asian countries that had pegged their currencies to the dollar were devastated by the rising dollar.[26] China held its ground tightening the range of movement of the Renminbi. The strong peg was a factor of critical importance in the resurgence of the region in the past decade. China's action was in fact welcomed by the US in that it helped limit the contagion effect of the Asian Crisis and preempt further debilitating rounds of devaluations.

China has, over the past decade, emerged as a major holder of US treasuries, actually surpassing Japan in 2008. Reserve holdings have grown from 1 percent GDP in 2000 to about 12 percent of GDP at the beginning of 2010.[27] More recently, before the collapse of the subprime market, Chinese banks had widened their portfolio to begin investing in the bonds of Fannie and Freddie. In fact this growing demand for US treasury and agency bonds has been cited as the source of the problem of global imbalances. In what might seem to be a case of the tail wagging the dog, the glut of savings searching for safe avenues of investment in China (and other Asian countries) has been blamed for the growing deficits of the US.

While China is a convenient scapegoat for the ills that plague the US economy, the savings glut narrative misses the real point. China's integration into the global economy has involved an export-led development strategy. This strategy, while yielding a rich dividend in terms of GDP growth and trade surpluses, forces China to intervene to keep its exchange-rate undervalued. Since the world wants to hold dollars and is not interested in holding renminbi, China is further constrained by the imperative to lend in dollars. So China ends up buying up treasury bills and, in effect, helping the US finance its deficit. China sterilizes the inflationary impact of buying these bonds by issuing domestic bonds (at a low interest rate) to mop up the spate in liquidity that is let loose. China is currently the largest creditor of the US government (the largest holder of US government debt) and is sitting on a mountain of US treasury bills. A collapse of the dollar would wipe out its asset base. The US and China are locked in a "balance of financial terror."

The deep structural changes that were engineered by the rising dominance of finance with the neoliberal backlash have promoted rising inequality and stagnant wages in the US. The US has been able to sustain consumption in the face of this growing inequality through the promotion of debt. The outsourcing of manufacture to low wage countries also helped flood the US markets with cheap imported consumer goods. This debt-fueled consumption binge of the US is the other side of the savings glut. The share of private consumption in China is 36 percent of GDP compared to 70 percent of GDP in the US.[28] The roots of the savings glut thus lie in the neoliberal growth model that has been promoted by the growing dominance of the US-led finance capital. The integration of developing countries into the circuit of the US-dominated finance capital has established a global division of labor where the manufacture of labor-intensive consumer goods has increasingly been off shored to developing countries especially in Asia. This pattern exacerbated the trade deficit of the United States.

This dominance, the centrality of the United States in global financial markets, is reflected in the fact that despite its net debtor position, the United States has consistently made money on its financial position (Figure 6.3).[29] The United States has been earning more income on its foreign asset holdings compared to what it pays out on its debts to the rest of the world. This return premium, which has been growing since the collapse of the Bretton Woods, reflects in a sense a return to the US's liquidity generating ability—the hegemony of the dollar.[30]

Figure 6.3. Net Receipts of Income from the Rest of the World (US$ Billions)

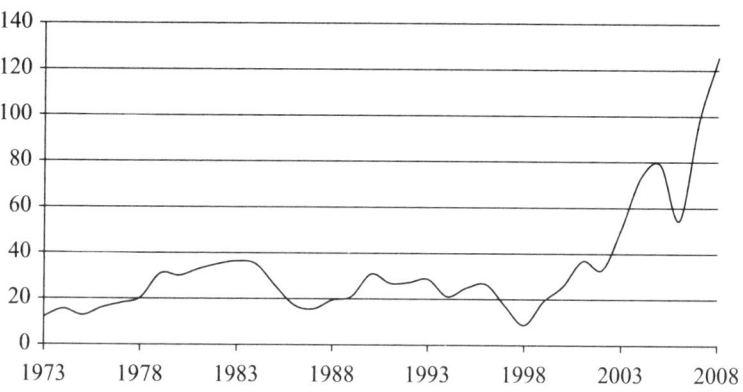

Source: Bureau of Economic Affairs.

CRACKS IN THE DOLLAR EDIFICE

The US is, in effect, the world banker. It has been able to tap into the surpluses of creditor countries in the periphery and recycle surpluses through financial markets to emerging markets in the periphery. Emerging markets have borne the brunt of speculative attacks that, in the final analysis, helped protect and preserve dollar hegemony through two decades of growing deficits and external debt. It is this mechanism that is at stake as under threat of unraveling in the wake of the Crisis.

An important part of the mechanism is the fact that the US earned more on its investments in the rest of the world than what it paid out on its borrowing (Figure 6.3). This "return premium" has remained positive through the past decades and has been rising since 1998, signifying the surge in the earnings of US investors from the rest of the world before the implosion. The dizzying

141

growth of financial innovations bred a structure of finance whose reach was global. The securitization of loans furthered the globalization of finance by creating financial products that were bought and sold globally. The US financial dominance allowed the US markets to draw funds from around the globe and seize opportunities for huge profits from its global investments, buying up a range of asset classes, including emerging market bonds and collateralized debt obligations. Nontraditional financial intermediaries such as private equity groups and hedge funds emerged as big global players growing by about 14 and 20 percent, respectively, in the first six years of this decade.[31]

At the same time the United States' share of global current account deficits has risen from 34 percent in 1995 to nearly around 65 percent in 2008. Global imbalances, the surge of liquidity, and the profusion of financial instruments and markets led to the increasing fragility of the financial system. The bubble was ready to burst.

There have also been important geopolitical changes taking place since the Asian Crisis. Developing countries, particularly in Latin America and Asia had transformed their current account deficits into surpluses. This was the outcome of hitching their economies to trade, specifically of primary commodities and labor-intensive manufacture. Scarred by the debilitating impact of the Crisis in Asia in 1997 and Russia in 1998, developing countries began accumulating a war chest of reserves in order to protect their economies from capital flight. Reserve holdings by developing countries rose to about US$ 3.7 trillion (37 percent of GDP) in 2007 (Figure 6.4).

These reserves were meant to afford protection against the threat of speculative flight. The stockpile of reserves meant that the markets in Latin America and Asia were now financing the bulk of US

Figure 6.4. Reserve Holdings and Current Account Balances (US$ Billions)

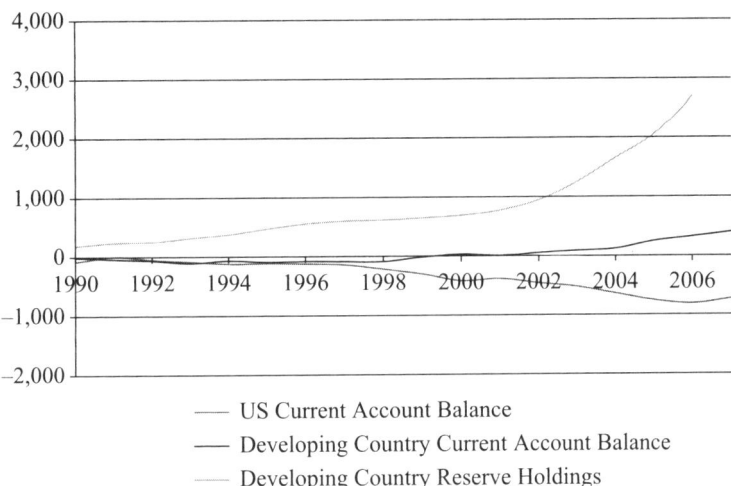

—— US Current Account Balance
—— Developing Country Current Account Balance
—— Developing Country Reserve Holdings

Source: Global Development Finance, Bureau of Economic Affairs.

deficits. These developing countries that had performed the role of a safety valve for the floating dollar standard through the 1980s and 1990s were, as a consequence, able to insulate their economies to a degree from financial crisis.

The revival of flows to the developing countries after 2002 has also been different in that inflows to the United States have also been increasing along with the surge in flows to emerging markets. After the collapse of the dot-com boom in 2002, when the relentless hunger for new frontiers for profits fueled the securitization boom and the housing bubble in the United States, buyers across the globe began investing in US mortgage-backed assets. The arm of predatory and speculative lending under the stewardship of US financial and corporate capital, turned toward US households instead of launching a new credit bubble in the emerging markets.

143

The mechanisms that had helped sustain the floating dollar standard were breaking down. The financial bubble in the US led to the emergence of a new pattern of dollar recycling that channeled capital flows from the surplus countries in the periphery toward US markets, including the subprime markets comprising the least credit worthy and poorest borrowers in the country. Buyers across the globe have been investing in these assets and over a trillion dollars of funds from around the globe, in particular from East Asia and the oil exporting countries, were swallowed up by the US subprime markets,[32] helping finance the purchase of homes all over the country and enabling the growth of consumption spending in the US. About 20 percent of the mortgage-backed securities and debt of Fannie and Freddie are owned by foreign investors.[33]

The exploding of the bubble with the collapse of the subprime mortgage market reflects mechanisms analogous to those that led to the debt crisis in the 1980s and the Asian meltdown in the nineties. It reflects the breakdown of the recycling mechanisms that exported fragility to the periphery through the 1980s and 1990s. Instead, these surpluses fueled the prodigious explosion of financial innovations on the back of the housing bubble in the US.

The unraveling of the subprime market posed a threat to the entire financial edifice as credit markets seized up. There was a sharp fall both in US investments abroad (which actually turned positive because of repatriation) and foreign investments in the US. The collapse of the financial markets also brought the proliferation of financial flows that had facilitated financial intermediation in the floating dollar standard to a halt (Figure 6.5).[34] These flows have been rising for the past three decades and plunged sharply as the subprime market unwound in 2007. In 2008, there was actually net inflow as foreign assets were liquidated and capital returned to the US.

Figure 6.5. The Collapse of Financial Intermediation

(Change in foreign holdings of US assets, Change in US holdings of assets abroad, and Current account deficit, in US$ billion)

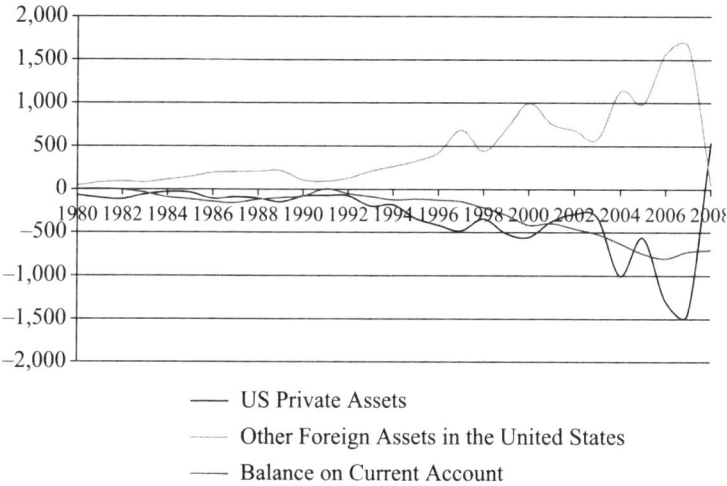

—— US Private Assets

—— Other Foreign Assets in the United States

—— Balance on Current Account

Source: Bureau of Economic Affairs.

FINANCE AND DOLLAR HEGEMONY

The credit crisis has revealed the vulnerability of an international financial system based on the growing debt of the US. Financialization and the explosion of private financial flows globally have helped the US preserve and establish its pivotal place at the center of the international financial markets, while the US deficit has continued to bloat. Private capital flows to emerging markets served as a safety valve mechanism enabling the export of crisis to the debtor periphery. This has allowed the easing of the external constraint, allowing the US to delay and evade the need for deflationary domestic adjustment while exacerbating global imbalances. As emerging markets began accumulating surpluses

145

and hoarding reserves, fragility instead of being displaced to the periphery came home to the core of advanced capitalist countries, precipitating the Crisis.

The implosion of the mechanisms underlying global liquidity precipitated a stampede to safety. The demand for US short-term treasury bills surged through 2008 (Figure 6.6). The US Treasury Bill is backed by perceived creditworthiness of the US state, and global dollar liquidity has been sustained on the basis of the demand for these treasury bills. This is the bedrock on which the burgeoning web of private financial flows has been erected over the past three decades.

The challenge for dollar hegemony would be to sustain the demand for treasuries even as the market for treasuries faces a glut as the US government's need for finance continues to expand. The increasing debt overhang may also undermine confidence in US

Figure 6.6. Foreign Holdings of US Treasury Bills

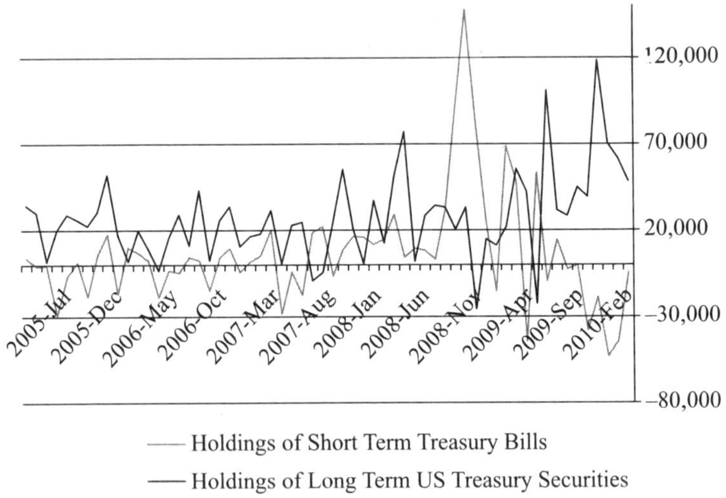

—— Holdings of Short Term Treasury Bills

—— Holdings of Long Term US Treasury Securities

Source: TIC.

Treasuries. Given that foreign holdings represent a significant proportion of the stockholdings of Treasuries, the collapse in Treasuries prices would manifest itself in a collapse of the US dollar as inflation soars and foreign demand for treasuries flags. This by itself does not necessarily imply a threat to dollar hegemony. The revival of investor confidence also manifested itself in a switch toward longer term treasury bonds. In the absence of an alternative to the dollar as the basis of international transactions what will sustain the continued hegemony of the dollar is the resurgence of global private financial flows.

The credit crisis has resulted in a collapse of the paper edifice of the bloated financial system to its fundamental monetary roots. The surge in global demand for US treasury bills following the collapse in investor confidence globally in the fall of 2008 manifests the same "clamor" for liquidity and safety in the form of world money that characterizes monetary crisis on a national scale. During the Great Depression, the spread of global contagion led to a stampede to gold, tightening monetary conditions in the US. The current crisis has paradoxically precipitated a demand for dollar liquidity and US treasury bills—the contemporary form of world money.

Marx, writing at a time when bullion assumed the role of "world money," highlighted the inherent deflationary bias of the international payments system with a contagion effect of payments crises among capitalist countries, when capital account flows move against these countries "in succession like volley firing."[35] These crises were, however, being transmitted within the core of advanced capitalist countries. The actual evolution of global capitalism has been shaped by the rising dominance of finance and the monetary liability or debt of a single dominant and imperialist country like the US has taken on the mantle of "world money."[36]

147

The Crisis unleashed by the collapse of the web of subprime-based securitization is in a sense a reflection of the contradictions of the dollar empire that was established in the postwar period.[37] The mechanisms of dollar liquidity have engendered the growing global imbalances and have been fueling increasing fragility. The current Crisis has brought the fragility home to the United States, its resolution will, however, have global repercussions—not unlike the volley firing that Marx wrote about.

Chapter 7

Aftershocks: The Crisis Goes Global

US Treasuries are the safe haven. For everyone, including China, it is the only option … Once you start issuing $1 trillion–$2 trillion] ... we know the dollar is going to depreciate, so we hate you guys but there is nothing much we can do.

— Luo Ping, Director General, China Banking Regulatory Commission, at the Global Association of Risk Management's 10th Annual Risk Management Convention, *Financial Times*, February 11, 2009

While the Crisis is in a very fundamental sense a crisis of dollar hegemony, this does not, however, imply that the Crisis heralds the end of the dominance of the dollar. Not only did the seizure of the credit machinery foment an insatiable thirst for dollars but the aftershock of the collapse of the subprime market in the United States has, in what is a strange twist of developments, also begun tearing apart the edifice that held together its main challenger—the eurozone.

As the contagion effects of the credit crisis spread across the financial system, the crisis that had initially appeared to be limited to the core of advanced capitalist countries came to engulf developing countries. Even though emerging markets were relatively less exposed to the market for mortgage-backed securities (though China, for instance, had begun to increase investments in agency bonds), they were deeply implicated in the integrated international financial system of the dollar standard. When the credit markets froze in the fall of 2008, foreign investors who had continued to flock to emerging markets through 2007 panicked. The ensuing stampede to the safe haven of US treasury holdings also triggered an immediate reversal of the capital flows to emerging markets. Net private capital flows to emerging markets declined to US$588 billion in 2008, less than half of their level in 2007 (US$1,247 billion).[1]

Debtor countries that relied on readily available capital to finance their current account deficits are particularly vulnerable. As it happened, these debtor countries were concentrated in the region around the edges of the European Union—Iceland and Eastern Europe, in particular. Eastern and Central Europe were among the hardest hit emerging market regions when financial flows dried up.

EASTERN EUROPE

The transition economies of Central Eastern European had enjoyed a decade of booming growth (on average 7 to 8 percent a year). Fueled by the concerted push toward deregulation, privatization, and financial liberalization, capital flowed into these countries. Lured by the prospect of being embraced by the European Union if they adopted the policies that conformed to the Maastricht criteria, these countries opened up their economies and began dismantling the public sector industrial establishment that had been the backbone of development in the region—a strategy that has been called "killing the geese." Opening up of the region enabled the closer integration of these economies through outsourcing at

150

the lower skill end of the global commodity chain. At the same time the banking sector, flush with funds from Western Europe, weaned itself off industry and turned toward household and real estate lending.[2]

While the region as a whole had current account deficits amounting to about 7 percent of GDP, the current account deficit had widened to as much as 21 percent of GDP in 2006 in Latvia, and around 10 to 16 percent of GDP in other Baltic countries and in Bulgaria and Romania. Reserve holdings for the region have been about 2 percent of GDP through the past few years (Figure 7.1). The region had also witnessed a huge inflow of private capital flows, which grew from 5 percent of GDP to nearly 9 percent

Figure 7.1. Eastern Europe: Increasingly Vulnerability (Percentage GDP)

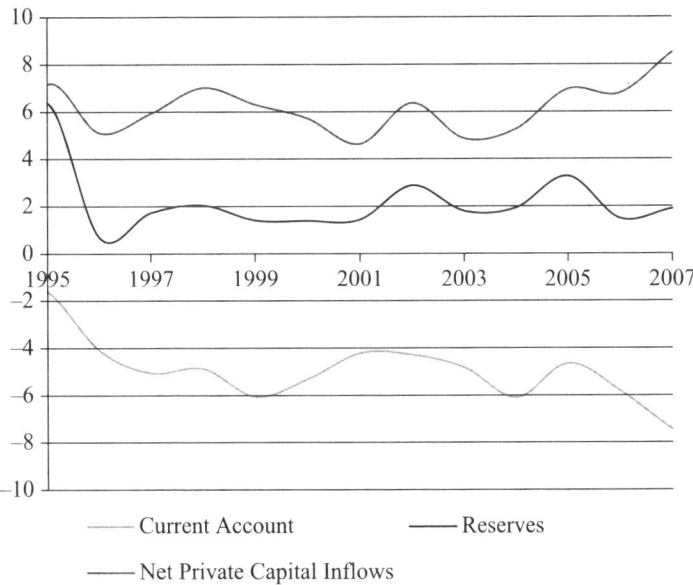

Source: Global Development Finance.

151

of GDP by 2006, as these transition economies boomed. More than one-third of all private capital flows to emerging markets targeted this region.[3] Soaring household borrowing was one of the key drivers of cross-border lending. The influx of cheap money sucked households into taking on more and more foreign currency debt (largely euro).

The Baltic countries (Estonia, Latvia, Lithuania) had about 67 percent of their foreign exchange loans denominated in foreign currency while the share for Central European countries (the Czech Republic, Hungary, Poland, Slovak) was 29 percent and that for the rest of Eastern Europe (Bulgaria, Croatia, Malta, Romania, and Turkey) was about 39 percent of their loans.[4] Compared to Latin America (with 18 percent of loans denominated in foreign currency) and Asia (with 6 percent of loans denominated in foreign currency), it would appear that the region was most afflicted by the "original sin" of incurring debt in a foreign currency. The Baltic countries with their currencies pegged to the euro were most at risk.

The debt indicators for the region were another warning sign. By 2006 the external debt to export earnings ratio (96 percent of GDP) and the debt to GDP ratio (40 percent) had surpassed that of Asia and even Latin America (Figure 7.2). By 2009 the region was beset by a classic emerging market crisis—the familiar pattern of a credit boom and burgeoning debt followed by the moment of panic as investor confidence evaporates. This panic brings down the currency as capital is pulled out. Private capital inflows that had tripled between 2005 and 2007 (from US$122 billion to a peak of US$393 billion) dwindled to a meager US$40 billion in 2009 with the credit crunch. Eastern Europe was, in fact, in the classic position of the debtor emerging market that had been the safety valve of the floating dollar standard, and parallels have

Figure 7.2. Debt Indicators for Eastern Europe, Latin America, and Asia (Percentage)

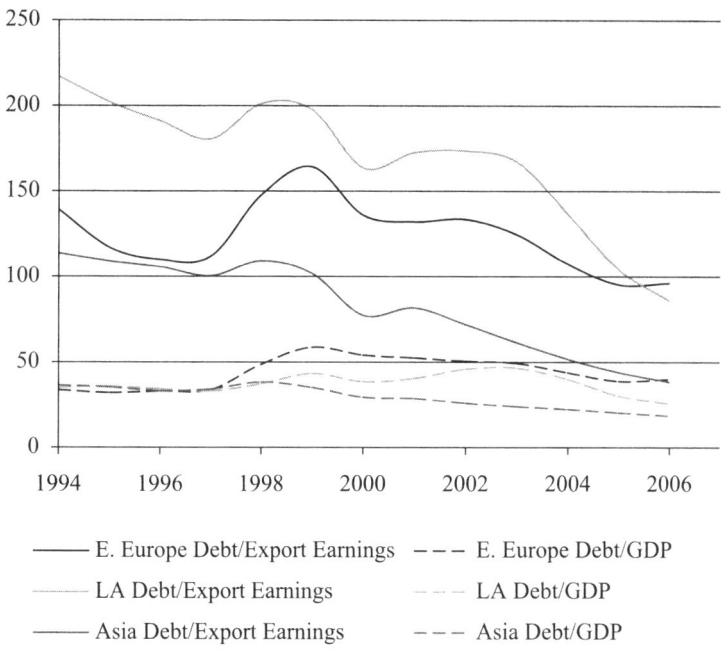

Legend:
——— E. Europe Debt/Export Earnings   – – – E. Europe Debt/GDP
——— LA Debt/Export Earnings   – – – LA Debt/GDP
——— Asia Debt/Export Earnings   – – – Asia Debt/GDP

Source: Global Development Finance.

been drawn between the crisis unfolding in the region and the Asian crisis in 1997.

A significant proportion (60 percent) of the region's long-term debt is in dollars. While the share of dollar debt is comparable to that of Asia (and lower than that of Latin America where the share is around 82 percent), the countries of the region are much more closely integrated to Western Europe and the eurozone. The euro component of long-term debt of the region at around 28 percent was much higher than that of both Latin America and Asia. Foreign-owned (primarily Western European) banks, led by Austrian

153

banks, accounted for 60 to 70 percent of total assets in the region.[5] These strong financial links also leave these West European banks vulnerable to risks of defaults and failures of their subsidiaries in the region. Cross-border lending and the spread of contagion to and through these dominant European banks pose a grave threat to the fragile recovery in Europe.

The European Union, which was also facing the full force of recessionary pressures, initially balked at extending support to Eastern Europe. As the crisis sharpened, threatening to bring down the exposed banks in Western Europe, the EU finally agreed to a €50 billion rescue package, doubling the limit on the existing provision for emergency support to EU members facing balance of payments crisis. Latvia, Hungary, and Romania drew on these funds. The crisis also gave an impetus within these countries toward embracing the euro as a way of protecting their economies.

THE ICELANDIC CRISIS

Iceland was one of the first countries to face the brunt of capital reversals. Iceland has seen the phenomenal growth of its banking sector as a result of liberalization and deregulation transforming itself from a nation most known for its fish industry to a banking haven. This was the much touted miracle of the Icelandic economy.

The total assets of the banking sector rose from 96 percent of GDP in 2000 to 800 percent of GDP in 2006. The panic that seized financial investors brought down this bloated banking sector. This was despite the fact that Icelandic banks were not particularly embroiled in the subprime mortgage-related markets. The unfavorable current account balance (16 percent of GDP in

2007) and the significantly negative net international investment position (about 120 percent of GDP) compounded the fragility of the country.[6] Iceland had accumulated massive short-term foreign currency liabilities. The majority of banks' revenues originate outside Iceland. Three large banks grew 20-fold between 2001 and 2008 and their short-term liabilities were 16 times greater than their foreign currency reserves.[7] Of the three large banks (Kaupthing, Landsbanki, and Glitnir) that dominated the banking sector, roughly half of Landsbanki's assets and two-thirds of the assets of Glitnir and Kaupthing were located outside of Iceland. Given that about 80 percent of all assets and 85 percent of all liabilities were denominated in foreign currency and that two-thirds of their funding comes mainly from the international wholesale markets, these banks were ripe for picking. The ripple effects of the credit crisis devastated the Icelandic banking sector pushing the economy to the brink of collapse.

The Krona plummeted and Iceland's government desperately sought a rescue. The banks were brought under government control. The interest rate was raised to 18 percent and severe austerity measures were launched. The financial tremors also lead to a change of political regime. By November 2009, a rescue program by international donors was set up with a loan of US$2.1 billion from IMF along with an additional US$3 billion from Nordic countries and US$5 billion from the UK, the Netherlands, and Germany. This US$10 billion plan was meant to help write off and restructure US$70 billion of debt.

The fate of the deposits from around Europe that were locked into stricken Icelandic banks—specifically in the Icesave accounts—the Internet banking operation of Landsbanki, became a contentious issue. The UK actually used anti-terror legislation to freeze Landsbanki's assets in the UK! In June 2009, the UK and the Netherlands agreed to a 15-year loan to a fund set up to bailout the depositors but extracted a government guarantee that would place Iceland on the hook for about one-third of its GDP. Even as Iceland tightened its belt to repay this loan, it stepped up the momentum on its application to join the European Union.

THE AEGEAN CRISIS

The crisis that engulfed the borders of the eurozone began drawing these regions closer into the fold of euro. This could have signaled a strengthening of the euro challenge to the dollar. This impetus to expanding the Eurozone has, however, taken place at a time when the tensions of the Eurozone are becoming evident after a decade of buoyant growth.

The rifts in monetary union were brought out into the open after the Panhellenic Socialist Movement (PASOK) party under George Papandreou rode a wave of discontent and won the snap elections in October 2009 amidst promises of increased social spending and the lifting of real wages. Within weeks the new regime was confronted not just with the impact of the economic crisis but also with the unearthing of deficits and debts much greater than those reported by the previous government. As against the earlier reported estimate of 3.7 percent of GDP, the deficits were revealed to be actually four times higher at 12.7 percent.

The sleight of hand by means of which the actual deficits were disguised involved the good offices of the same investment banks that were at the epicenter of the implosion of the financial system. In 2001 when Greece was struggling to meet the stringent criteria that were conditions for its entry to the Eurozone, Goldman Sachs stepped in with creative arrangements that allowed the

Greek government to borrow cash upfront in return for government payments in the future, without having to record these transactions as accumulating liabilities in government accounts. Classically named entities such as Aeolos and Ariadne were created in order to take debt off the government books, but, in return, the Greek government traded away rights to future incomes. "Aeolos" was deployed to pledge away future airport fees while Ariadne claimed revenues from state lotteries. The magic accounting is such that these loans got recorded as sales helping Greece disguise the full extent of its indebtedness and smoothen its path to the EMU. Goldman Sachs also pocketed about US$300 million in fees for arranging these transactions.[8]

Greece, of course, was not alone in resorting to SPVs and derivatives to mask its debt. Italy when faced with the prospect of being denied entry to the EMU on the grounds of fiscal profligacy, undertook yen–lira swaps brokered by J.P. Morgan in 1997 with off market rates that undervalued the lira. These transactions allowed the Italian state to take on debt while representing it as a hedge for a yen bond that would mature in 1998. Italy was effectively taking a cash advance from J.P. Morgan in 1997 against an expected foreign exchange profit in 1998.[9] Fancy footwork by Wall Street bankers brokering these deals allowed the state to transform debt into a hedge using derivatives. In fact Goldman Sachs is reported to have offered to create new derivatives based on future earnings from the Greek healthcare system to transmute the debt of this sector into assets in November after the first rumblings of concern about Greek debt![10]

With the revelations of the full extent of indebtedness of Greece, the credit rating agencies got into the act and downgraded Greek sovereign bonds. By April 2010, Greek bonds had plummeted to junk status. Yields on government bonds soared, reaching 7.25 percent on 10-year government bonds in December 2010, the highest level since 1999. The panic was fueled by the surge in short selling of Greek bonds. Short selling involves the sale of a security that has been borrowed with the intention of buying an identical security at a lower price and returning it to the lender. A very lucrative way of manipulating prices and pocketing the margin, such short selling often involved the sales transactions where the seller did not actually even possess the security! Apart from such "naked" short selling, the investors were also betting on an imminent default by Greece, by taking out credit default swaps as insurance against such an outcome (even without necessarily owning any Greek bonds). The sellers (often pension funds) earned an insurance premium but the hedge fund that bought the insurance without having any stake in Greek sovereign debt would make a hefty profit if Greece defaulted. The surge in such credit default swaps exacerbated the financial crisis in Athens by panicking investors. This is exactly the same scenario that toppled AIG. The investment banks in the meantime also pocketed the fee for brokering these transactions!

All this speculative activity helped drive up the spreads on the credit default swaps on Greek debt (that measure the cost to insure debt against default), reflecting perceptions of greater riskiness and the higher cost of insurance.[11] There were growing complaints that some ruthless investors were manipulating these markets to deliberately sow panic, so that they can benefit through clever trades. So Wall Street played a critical role not just in facilitating the masking of deficits in Greece using the same tactics that Enron and Lehman had employed to airbrush their books but also in whipping up the hysteria and investor panic that precipitated the crisis in Greece.

The bonanza of cheap credit that had flowed into Greece suddenly dried up. At the same time the downgrading of Greek bonds meant that Greek commercial banks could not avail of the liquidity facilities of the European Central bank by posting government bonds as collateral, exacerbating the credit crunch. The focus shifted to government profligacy and the Greek government was faced with the prospect of a being unable to cough up when its debt fell due in May 2010. The country's public debt that was around 114 percent in 2009 was set to jump to more than 135 percent of GDP. About two-thirds of Greece's public debt is held by foreigners with the UK and Ireland holding 23 percent, France 11 percent, Germany, Austria, and Switzerland about 9 percent, and Benelux countries another 6 percent.[12] Gross external debt—both private and public sector owed to foreign creditors—was nearly 150 percent of GDP.[13]

Wall Street stepped in to help orchestrate a rescue. Goldman Sachs, the bank that had helped Greece camouflage its debt, and that had been rumored (in collusion with the Paulson Hedge Fund) to have played a role in the speculative attacks on Greek bonds that fueled the surge in rates, now assumed a lead role in advising the Greek government on the sale of its bonds (including a reported attempt to sell bonds to China that fell through).[14]

The "profligacy" of the Greek government and its leaking tax infrastructure has been held to blame as the cause of the collapse of the market for government debt. A lot of the ire has been directed at excessive social sector spending, in particular on pensions and retirement benefits. The image projected is that of a workforce that has been propped up by a bloated public sector and the early retirement age policies.[15] And yet, workers in Greece work the longest annual working hours within the EU—a total of 2,120 hours in 2008, compared to 1,430 hours for German workers and

1,544 hours for French workers.[16] The average age at which workers leave the workforce in Greece is not significantly different from that in Germany and the expected lifespan after retirement is also not very different.[17]

The problems that Greece faces reflect the wider problems posed by integration of peripheral European countries into the eurozone. The crisis has not been limited to Greece. Bond markets in Portugal, Italy, Spain, and Ireland have also been facing rough weather fueled by fears of rising sovereign debt. The Greek crisis has morphed into a crisis for the Eurozone that continues to thwart the fragile hopes of global recovery.

IMBALANCES OF THE EUROZONE

The project of the Eurozone welds together countries such as Greece, Portugal, Spain, Italy, and Ireland with a core centered around Germany and France. At the heart of the strength of the euro are the surpluses of the German economy. The surpluses of Germany are mirrored by outflows of bank lending and foreign direct investment to the rest of the eurozone. Countries in the periphery of the eurozone have, in contrast, been running up deficits, and, having joined the euro at high exchange rates, cannot use devaluation as a tool to manage their trade deficits. And so the adoption of the euro has buttressed the surpluses of Germany while firmly entrenching the deficits of countries like Greece and Spain (Figure 7.3).

About 75 percent of Germany's trade (and 90 percent of its surplus) was with 27 EU countries and 38 percent of its trade (60 percent surplus) with the other Eurozone members.[18] Exports which comprised nearly 50 percent of Germany's GDP in 2008 (and 40

Figure 7.3. Imbalances within the Eurozone (Current Account Balance US$ Billion)

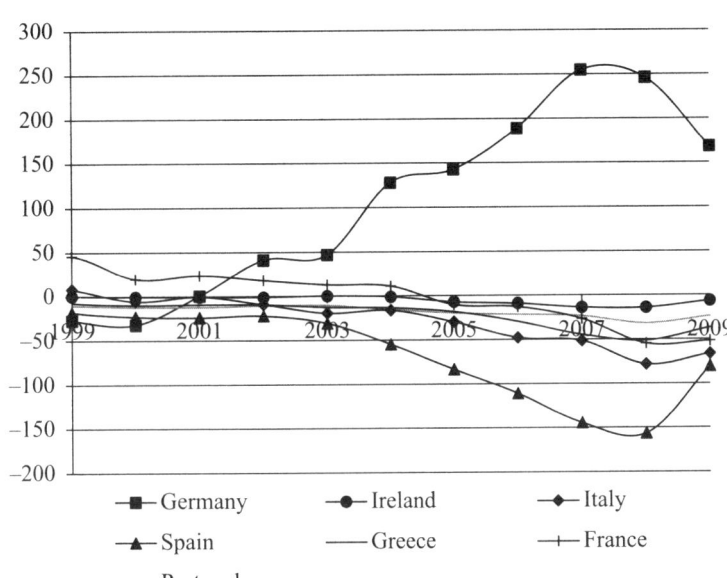

Germany — Ireland — Italy — Spain — Greece — France — Portugal

Source: International Financial Statistics.

percent in 2009) were the principal source of demand and dynamism of the German economy as domestic consumption growth remained stagnant. There was a temporary reprieve with the reunification, but since the inception of the euro, Germany has been relocating cheap products to Eastern Europe and curbing internal demand with severe wage repression.

The export competitiveness of Germany, in turn, is derived in large part from the intensive restructuring of the labor market that has enabled a drastic clamping down on labor costs. Reforms have imposed greater flexibility in labor contracts, reduced social contributions and unemployment benefits, and raised the retirement age. Outsourcing chunks of the labor process to Eastern and Central

Europe has further helped keep wage costs from rising. Since 1995, nominal unit labor costs for Germany have been relatively stagnant while costs in Greece, Portugal, and Spain increased by 50 to 60 percent. In the same period, the productivity of labor in Germany rose by about 20 percent, growing more slowly than Greece, Ireland, and Portugal.[19] The competitiveness of Germany depends on its success in keeping down unit labor costs relative to peripheral countries in the Eurozone (Figure 7.4).

Figure 7.4. Index of Unit Labor Costs (100 = 2000)

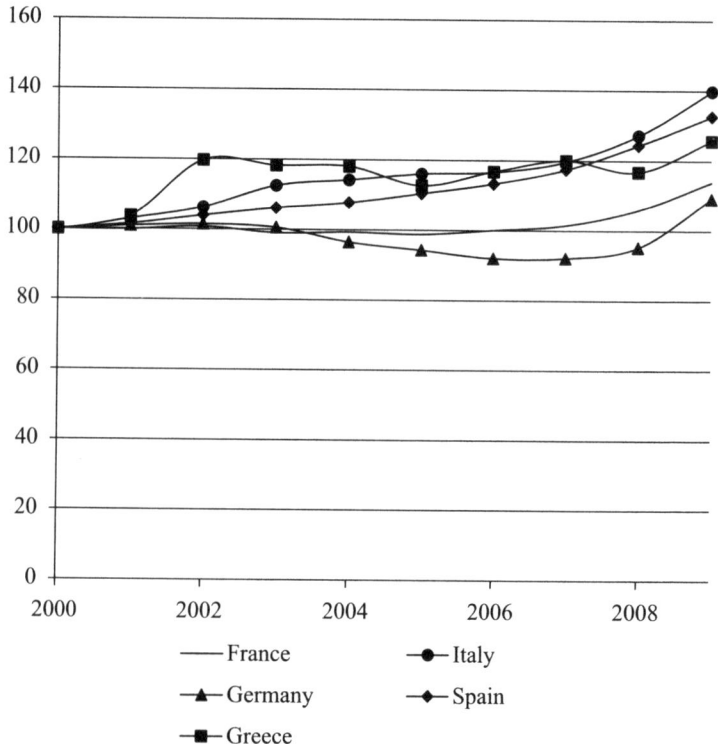

Source: Eurostat.

The relative stagnation in unit labor costs in Germany has to be seen in the context of the higher share of labor costs in the value of output in Germany when compared to the peripheral Eurozone countries (Figure 7.5). Peripheral countries whose currency is tied to the euro do not have the option of devaluing their currency in order to restore competitiveness; instead, they are being led down the path of squeezing workers and adopting the more stringent cuts on social spending. This, despite the fact

Figure 7.5. Share of Labor Costs (As a Percentage of Output)

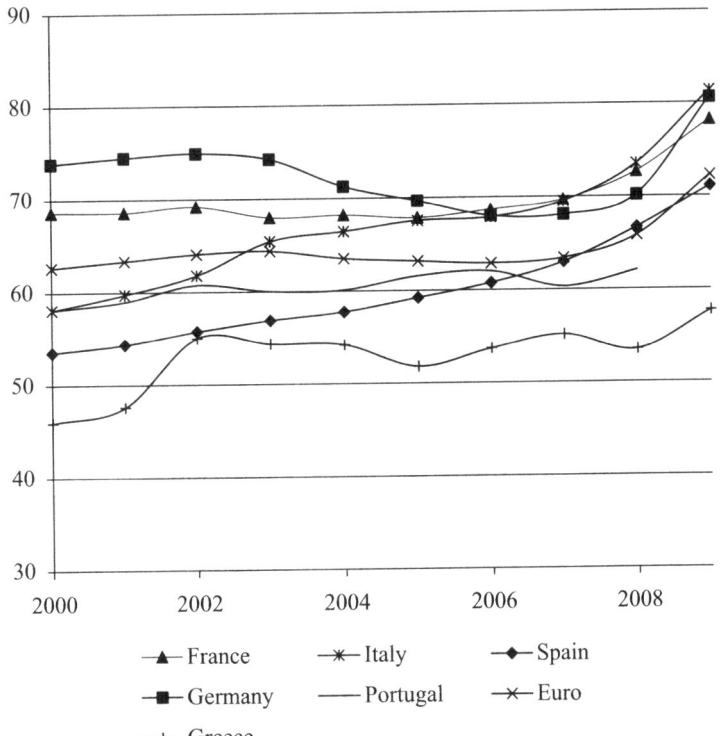

Source: Eurostat.

that average compensation and the share of labor costs remains lower in these countries compared to Germany. Labor market reform serves the larger agenda of monetary integration, neoliberal reform in the Eurozone, and is fostering the conditions for a race to the bottom.[20]

The adoption of the euro had granted these entrants to the Eurozone access to cheap money hitched to the low interest rates that the European Central Bank (ECB) offered. So banks in the region could borrow at the low interest rate that ECB has been offering and then acquire higher yield securities. The incentives were clearly skewed toward piling on greater and greater debt. This bonanza fueled the property bubble in Spain and Ireland and debt fueled consumption in Greece and Portugal.[21]

In macroeconomic terms, the peripheral countries had been financing their current account deficits with capital inflows and rising private sector deficits. While export demand sustained the German economy, growth in the rest of the eurozone has been hitched to credit-fueled demand within the zone itself. With the onset of the crisis, the overextended private sectors began to cutback and retrench. As the private sector began hoarding and the recession continued to weigh on trade deficits, the offset for these private surpluses would spill over in the form of rising public deficits.[22] The downgrades of the credit ratings of Spain, Portugal, Greece, and Ireland and the spike in rates on their sovereign debt following the crisis brought to a standstill the decade of cheap credit, as the panic in the bond markets spread.

European banks are the most exposed with about two-thirds of the region's debt being concentrated in cross-border flows within the region. Spain, Ireland, Portugal, and Greece owe nearly US$1.6 trillion to banks in the 16-country Eurozone, either in the form of government debt or credit to companies and individuals

164

in the four countries. A big chunk of these claims belonged to French and German banks. German and French banks thus carry a combined US$900 billion in exposure (to both public and private sectors) to countries on the Eurozone's vulnerable periphery: Greece, Portugal, Ireland, and Spain.[23] French banks had lent US$493 billion to Spain, Greece, Portugal, and Ireland by the end of 2009 while German banks had lent US$465 billion, according to the report by the Bank for International Settlements.[24] The largest non-Euro area holders of claims on the above four public sectors were Japanese and UK banks (US$23 billion and US$22 billion, respectively). Government debt, however, accounts for a smaller part of Euro area banks' exposures to the "at risk" countries than claims on the private sector. The joint foreign claims of banks headquartered in the Eurozone on the public sectors of Greece, Ireland, Portugal, and Spain (US$254 billion) amounted to approximately 16 percent of their combined overall exposures to these countries.[25]

These peripheral countries also have significant cross-borrowings amongst themselves.[26] A default in Greece could set off a domino effect of collapses in countries in the Eurozone. The dependence of Germany—the engine of the Eurozone economy—on exports and the vulnerabilities of the bank-dependent financial system of the Eurozone would propagate the impact of a crisis that had its epicenter in the US into a crisis that threatens to undermine the basis of the euro. The demand for exports waned after the crisis and the flight of deposits from the Euro periphery to core banks has burst the bubble that fueled peripheral economies. So the crisis of the mechanisms underpinning the dollar standard has transformed into a crisis for the euro.

Even before the collapse of Bear Stearns, major banks across the Atlantic (including the French Bank BNP Paribas and the German

IKB *Deutsche Industrie Bank*) were caught in the vortex of the imploding subprime mortgage market in the US. Two years later, German and French banks in particular, found themselves heavily implicated in the public debt of peripheral Eurozone countries. The euro plunged sharply, following the "flash crash" on May 7, 2010, when default fears, high frequency trading, and what might have been a technology malfunction led to widespread panic and plummeting of the US stock markets. The fault lines of the Euro project have been exposed. The exposure of insolvency of large sections of the German and French banking system could precipitate a banking crisis at the core of the Eurozone and jeopardize the incipient recovery in Germany.

THE EURO CRISIS

The Maastricht treaty that was signed in 1992 had set the stage for the creation of the euro. The project of the single currency had been pushed under French and German initiatives in order to forge a monetary union in Europe. The center piece of the European Monetary Union that came into effect in 1999 is the European Central Bank. The ECB has provided significant amounts of liquidity to the financial systems of the euro region, and extended support to the rescue of Eastern European countries through the crisis. ECB lending grew from around €450 billion before the collapse of Lehman to about €880 billion in June 2010. The recessionary forces unleashed by the global crisis have, however, brought into sharp focus the divergences within the monetary union. Two years down the line, the costs of stimulating the contracting economies, propping up the flailing financial sector and the flagging tax revenues took their toll on public finances. The financial crisis morphed into a debt crisis. This is, of course, the standard pattern of financial crisis historically.[27]

There is, however, a difference between the public debt of the US and that of Europe. The US treasury bill is backed by the creditworthiness of the US state, and there is therefore a deep and liquid market for US treasury bills. There is no comparable market for public debt that enjoys the monetary backing of the European Central bank at the Eurozone level. Instead, each member issues its own sovereign debt and the market for public debt is fragmented by differences in risk perceptions. Thus when a full-fledged credit crunch had the financial markets in its grip, it was toward US treasury bills that investors flocked. The ECB had to draw on dollar swap lines in order to pump liquidity into the financial system in Europe.

A crucial stumbling block for the functioning of the monetary union is the absence of a mechanism for fiscal coordination. Monetary policy is centralized and kept insulated from national political imperatives (the principle of central bank autonomy) but fiscal policy lies in the hands of national governments and is subject not just to political constraints but also to the tyranny of the bond markets. Under the convergence criteria of the Growth and Stability Pact (the agreement that enforced fiscal discipline on members of European Monetary Union) the budget deficit of member countries has to be kept below 3 percent of GDP and public debt lower than 60 percent of GDP. This pact was the bulwark that was supposed to ensure harmonization of policy within the European Union and ensure the commitment to targeting inflation.

As the European economies face the impact of the global contraction, the difficulties of coordinating a euro-wide stimulus among the different states and the antigrowth bias of the Growth and Stability Pact is proving to be an obstacle to recovery in the region. The lowering of interest rates had helped inject liquidity into the region as financial markets ground to a halt in 2008. However, the varying capacity of member countries to pursue independent rescue plans after the crisis has also stoked divergences in the interest rate spread on their government bonds. The ECB does not have the tools to control the financial markets or intervene in the collapsing markets for public debt. The ECB, unlike other central banks, cannot regulate liquidity in the region through buying and selling of government bonds since it is not allowed under the statutes to buy sovereign bonds of its members. Commercial banks in the member countries can, however, extend liquidity by borrowing at the low prevailing interest rate from the ECB against investment grade debt posted with the bank.

With the onset of the crisis, lending (in particular by French and German banks) to peripheral Eurozone countries dried up, even as the economies of the region faced the consequences of recession. In Greece, the shipping and tourism industries, the mainstay of the economy, faced a severe downturn. The bubbles that had sustained Ireland and Spain burst. But once the debt of a Eurozone member falls to near junk status, the ECB will no longer accept these bonds as collateral. The spigot of credit flows is turned off. This is the prospect that faced Greece and other Eurozone countries as their debt was downgraded. In March 2010, the European Central Bank abandoned its plan to raise the required credit rating for accepting bonds as collateral in its liquidity operations, ensuring that the Greek banks were not left out in the cold. There was, however, no perceptible breach in the buyer's strike of Greek bonds.

The mechanisms of the ECB are also not engineered to address financial crisis. Its sole mandate, enshrined in the Maastricht Treaty, is to keep a rein on inflation and maintain price stability. The "no bail out clause" of the Maastricht treaty explicitly prohibits the European community or members of the Eurozone from performing "lender of resort" rescues of countries or institutions facing a crisis. So while the ECB actions helped to prop up liquidity as the subprime crisis erupted, the rescue of failing institutions was initially left to national governments.

Germany in particular was reluctant to support a "bail out" of Greece without a firm commitment that Greece would set its house in order. The prospect of an IMF rescue of a Eurozone country was also not palatable. So when Greece opened negotiations with the IMF, the European Council stepped forward to set up a €45 billion package in coordination with the IMF in April 2010. This was after Greece had announced three austerity packages in about five months, without any effect in assuaging the financial markets. The fund proved inadequate to reassure the markets and the resources allocated were increased to €110 billion in May. The condition for this support was a commitment by the Greek government to cut its deficit from nearly 13 percent to less than 3 percent by 2014. As a signal of its commitment, Greece announced severe cutbacks, freezing salaries, slashing allowances and pensions for civil servants, and raising consumer taxes.

As the crisis continued to spiral out of control and hit the markets in Portugal, Spain, Italy, and Ireland too, the ECB was pushed into taking the unprecedented step of buying European government bonds in the open markets in May 2010 when trading had nearly come to a halt. This is a small step toward acknowledging the role of the central bank in providing a market for government debt when private investors turn skittish. However, anti-inflationary imperatives and the strong resistance to any erosion of central bank insulation from regional political dynamics continue to haunt the ECB. Even though European economies faced massive unemployment (which is, for instance, more than 20 percent in

Spain), the neoliberal strait jacket of the mandate of the Maastricht treaty and the Stability Pact continues to shape the response of the ECB.

After many months of wrangling, the EU and the IMF finally agreed in May 2010 to pledge nearly US$1 trillion (€750 billion) in aid and debt guarantees for Eurozone governments to help stave off speculative attacks on member countries of the Eurozone. The European Commission would raise and provide €60 billion under the same emergency support arrangements that it had deployed in Eastern Europe—the European Financial Stabilization Mechanism. The big leap was the creation of a temporary SPV—the European Financial Stability Facility (EFSF)—with member countries contributing to a war chest of €440 billion to provide loans as a backstop to countries that were being shunned by the markets. This fund would raise money by issuing bonds that would be fully guaranteed by the member states (other than the country seeking help) and would function as a separate entity under the joint share ownership of national governments.

Apart from the bureaucratic hiccups in making the fund (which will be housed in Luxemburg and not in Brussels where the ECB is headquartered) operational, the response of the markets to its bonds is still to be tested. The real issue is that these bonds, which are backed by the "joint" credibility of the Euro-states, cannot match the US Treasury Bill as a safe haven asset backed by US fiscal authorities. This initiative, which hopes to quell market fears by invoking the illusion of lending power—the proverbial "big bazooka," does signal an attempt to create some semblance of a safety net for countries facing speculative attacks. The central bank, however, remains constrained by its narrow mandate to keep inflation in check and the limited ability of the ECB to actively intervene in the markets in support of financial stability. In the absence of a unified or pooled market for euro-level debt, the dollar remains the ultimate source of liquidity in the eurozone.

The extension of the Federal Reserve dollar swap lines to other central banks in October 2008 had been crucial in enabling the ECB to prop up liquidity by gaining access to dollar funds after the collapse of Lehman. These swap lines were reactivated in May 2010 amidst fears that the debt crisis in the Eurozone would ricochet on markets in the US. The total exposure by US institutions to Spain, Greece, Portugal, and Ireland at US$176 billion is much lower than that of German and French banks.[28] This exposure is, however, concentrated within the top 10 US banks, explaining why the Federal Reserve felt compelled to enter the breach, even though disquiet about its ballooning balance sheets had risen sharply. Both the panic and the revival of the swap lines highlight the constraints that the Euro faces as a challenge to the dollar.

As the crisis unfolded, the neoliberal model of finance fell into disrepute and the tenets of the Washington Consensus were brought into question. As the economies of core countries teetered on the verge of collapse, for a while, governments put a brake on the neoliberal policy machine and adopted fiscal stimulus plans to resuscitate their economies. This was in stark contrast to the response to the crisis faced by developing countries in the 1980s and 1990s, when the conditionality attached to the IMF's loans enforced brutal measures of fiscal austerity. The crisis in Europe's periphery has emerged as the vantage point for a new neoliberal backlash. The havoc that bond markets have wrought on government's capacity to sustain their recovery efforts is stoking fears of sovereign debt defaults and preparing the ground for a renewed assault on the nascent consensus on the need for fiscal stimulus.

THE RETURN OF AUSTERITY

The IMF had played a very marginal role in the initial stages of the financial crisis. The experience of the Asian crisis, where the IMF had stepped in to rescue the afflicted countries with money tied to extremely savage spending cuts that prolonged and intensified the contraction and hardship have left these countries with a deep aversion to these programs. These countries began acquiring surpluses and stockpiling reserves as an insurance against crisis and the need to turn to the IMF. The unfolding crisis did not, however, leave the "surplus" countries in Asia and Latin America unscathed.

The export-led growth strategy of surplus countries in the periphery ties these economies closely to the appetite for imports of the US economy. The bursting of the commodity boom after the fall of Lehman and the buildup of recessionary forces in the US and the EU had a direct impact on the current account surpluses of primary goods and manufacture exports of developing countries. Russia, Korea, Brazil, Singapore, and Mexico—all saw their reserves erode. China, too, faced a steep fall in its export earnings. In November 2008 the IMF announced a new Short-Term Liquidity Facility that would provide "no strings loans," of as much as double the quotas for three months to countries that were deemed to be "good performers" facing temporary shortfalls in liquidity. To qualify for such access, a nation would need to have low inflation, moderate levels of foreign debt, small current account deficits, and sound public finances. The changed situation of qualifying countries (especially those in Asia and Latin America that have suffered the stigma and stringent conditionality associated with IMF loans in the past) is evident in the fact that this special facility initially had no takers.

172

It was in Eastern Europe, in efforts coordinated with the European Union, that the IMF, once again, found a role. As the crisis began to enmesh Eastern and Central Europe, countries in the region (including Iceland, Hungary, Ukraine, Romania, Belarus, Latvia, and Serbia) turned to the IMF for help. The IMF had, by February 2009, earmarked a bailout of about US$55 billion to these countries tied to the familiar package of fiscal tightening and monetary austerity that involve freezing public sector wages, pensions, and other social transfers ostensibly to improve government finances and attract foreign investors.

As countries in the Eurozone fell prone to investor panic and the specter of debt default, the IMF found itself involved in the rescue of a western European country for the first time since its intervention in Italy and the UK in the 1970s. For the three decades before this crisis, countries that went bust were the smaller, emerging market nations. The IMF has contributed about US$40 billion to the US$147 billion rescue package for Greece. At about 32 times the Greek quota at the IMF, this bailout dwarfs all previous bailouts engineered by the IMF. To get a sense of the scale, compare this contribution with the IMF's US$28 billion contribution to the US$79 billion bailout of South Korea in 1997–98 (what was, at the time, one of the biggest rescue efforts organized by the US IMF and the World Bank), which was about 20 times the country's quota.[29] The scale of the Greek rescue has shattered previous limits and marks an entry to new and unchartered territory.[30] With the provision of about €250 billion to the rescue fund set up by the EU to deal with the European debt crisis, the stakes of the IMF (and by proxy the US) in the region has been consolidated.

The Eurozone sovereign debt crisis has given a renewed impetus both to a greater role for the IMF and to turning back the paradigm shift in favor of Keynesian programs. Germany has been reluctant to finance what it sees as the fiscal follies and financial profligacy of other Eurozone members. When the prospect of the crisis in the euro periphery bringing down German banks compelled an emergency response, the first package cobbled together by the EU and the IMF (and the US) made the enforcement of fiscal cutbacks, scaling back public pension plans, healthcare and education, privatization, and a restructuring of labor markets, its core condition. The proposed changes in labor market regulations would weaken workers' bargaining power, leading to cuts in wages, even as the cuts in spending exacerbate unemployment. The fabric of the safety net that has been the centerpiece of European capitalist economies, including unemployment and retirement benefits, are being ripped apart by this policy assault. Greece, Portugal, Spain, Italy, and Ireland—all announced savage slashes to their budgets. The cuts have led to drops in GDP growth, and a surge in unemployment in these countries, further pushing up debt–GDP ratios. These countries are thus being left even more vulnerable to the tyranny of bond markets and the trauma of deflation.

The crisis that began with the collapse of the housing bubble in the US had turned its attention to the weakness of the Anglo-Saxon model of development. There is an irony in the fact that two years later the model under assault is that of Social Europe. The power of finance has not been curbed. The rescue—and the firepower unleashed in bringing down social spending and squeezing workers—are in fact a bailout for banks and finance. There is a reason why deflation is being imposed rather than a restructuring that would ease the burden of debt on these countries. Such restructuring could take the form of "haircuts" in the rates that bond holders receive or of partial write-offs or postponements of debt repayment. Such a path would have forced finance to bear some of the costs of coping with the crisis that it unleashed. But finance continues to hold states and public policy to ransom with the threat of pulling the plug if anything shakes its fragile confidence. And what restores confidence are measures that ensure its earnings are dynamic. And so the logic of finance is pushing Europe down the road of fiscal austerity in order to protect and preserve the earnings and profits of finance while passing on the costs to the working poor in these countries.

There are signs that this revival of the neoliberal juggernaut is pressing against its political limits. Latvia, the poster child of "how to successfully swallow your reform medicine," has seen its GDP fall by about 22 percent between 2007 and 2009, and unemployment rise to about 24 percent after it slashed its fiscal deficit from 12 percent to 5 percent of GDP by imposing huge wage and spending cuts. With the support for its coalition government fraying, the legislators have passed a bill to cut value-added tax in defiance of the IMF conditionality.

The disbursement of the successive tranches of the 2009 IMF package to Ukraine went through many delays over the implementation of the conditionality around a balanced fiscal budget. The final tranche was suspended in the Spring of 2010 when Ukraine went ahead and stepped up its social spending and raised minimum wages and pensions. A new loan package of US$15 billion has been negotiated with the new Yanukovych government in July 2010. Funds were again frozen in February 2011 when the new government did not comply with the demand to raise utility bills. A third lending negotiation is now underway.

Iceland has been juggling the demands to make good the losses of European depositors (in the controversial Icesave accounts) on the one hand and the pressing urgency of addressing the needs of the Icelandic people who were facing the full force of an acute recession. A legislation passed in August 2009—the Icesave bill—sought to repay the UK and the Netherlands for more than US$5 billion that had disappeared in the Icesave accounts, but limited the repayment to a ceiling based on the GDP growth. The UK and the US continued to wrestle over these terms and the threat that the US$10 billion aid package would get jeopardized led to amendments to the bill that were more favorable to the creditor banks. But the public furor that ensued has compelled President Ólafur Grímmson to put the issue to a referendum. The referendum overwhelmingly rejected the terms. Iceland has, since then, embarked on a path of applying the brakes on finance and shoring up its social safety net. By 2012 most of its loans had been repaid, its unemployment had come down to around 6 percent, and its growth prospects looked brighter than the rest of Europe. Iceland is also the first country to launch a criminal trial against its former Prime Minister Geir H. Haarde over his role in the collapse of the banking system, convicting him in the end of "criminal negligence."

Greece, Portugal, Spain, and Italy, too, have faced successive storms of protests as the governments have moved forward with harsh measures to appease the financial markets. French workers have come out in huge marches to protest the plan to raise the retirement age. In Greece, through the summer of 2011, farmers blockaded key junctions, striking workers took to the streets in large numbers, the public squares were occupied, and schools, public offices, and transport were shut down in waves of popular resistance to the draconian policies that were integral to the first bailout package. In October 2011, when Prime Minster Papandreou failed to follow through on the promised referendum on the terms of the bailout package, under pressure from the European Union, the European Central Bank, and the International Monetary Fund, he faced a storm of protests and had to resign. The former banker Lucas Papademos was put in place to implement the new austerity measures and shepherd a second €130 billion bailout package, along with a ratcheting up of austerity. A dramatic last minute agreement on debt restructuring in March 2011 forced the banks and funds to accept losses of as much as 75 percent on their holdings of Greek bonds along with a further tightening of the austerity screws. Output and demand have continued to fall. Wages fell by around 7 percent in both 2010 and 2011 (with a similar fall projected in 2012) and GDP by nearly as much as much as in this same period.[31] With tax revenues declining in the face of this contraction and debt repayment constituting the first claim on these dwindling tax revenues, it is not surprising that these rescues are failing to resolve the debt crisis and to dispel fears of default.

Unemployment crossed 20 percent in 2012. The Greek populace that has been subjected to the devastating burden of rescuing finance delivered a clear indictment against this austerity agenda in the two round elections held in the summer of 2012 where both the dominant parties—the socialist PASOK and the center right New Democracy Party—saw their mandate significantly eroded and SYRIZA, an alliance of the left opposed to the conditions of the bailout package blazed to the second place. The New Democracy Party led by Antonis Samaras finally cobbled a coalition with PASOK and is now engaged in pushing through further spending cuts and privatization of public assets in the face of a continuing storm of protests.

In the meanwhile, the central problems of the imbalance at the heart of the Eurozone—the persistence of the German surpluses, its reliance on exports as an engine of growth and the regressive distributional basis of this regime—are not being addressed. The relentless slashing of spending by Eurozone countries has failed to calm market sentiment. The European Central Bank has resorted to extraordinary measures to revive lending. In December 2011, the European Central Bank began making three-year loans to banks directly at a 1 percent interest rate against acceptable government and private securities—the Long-Term Refinancing Operation. A second similar extraordinary lending operation was launched three months later in March 2012. The Eurozone is also slowly creaking its way toward creating the European Stability Mechanism (ESM)—a permanent bail out fund (in place of the temporary EFSF) empowered to buy bonds from beleaguered sovereigns. In September 2012 the European Central Bank announced a new program—Outright Monetary Transactions—to be executed through the ESM–EFSF, to buy bonds of up to three years maturity with more relaxed collateral requirements. This European version of the "credit easing" and "lender of last resort" interventions, however, only buys time. It does not address the contradictions at the heart of the euro. Nor have they been successful in restoring investment and lending in the face of the privatization, deregulation, and the brutal slashing of government spending. In fact the bond-buying initiatives come with a host of conditionalities that enforce austerity and would exacerbate the prospect of default by eroding the capacity of states to repay loans, while putting the central bank on line for the accumulation of toxic assets on its balance sheets.

And so, with the Eurozone in disarray, and confidence in the euro at its lowest since its inception, the dominance of the dollar remains, for the time being, unchallenged. The US Treasury Bill remains the anchor of the global financial system. The privileged role of the dollar continues to provide the US an extremely flexible credit line that allows it to run up deficits simply by issuing dollar debt. For this to work, however, the US needs buyers for its treasury bonds. This is where the Chinese central bank steps in. The US agenda of refashioning the post-crisis world in a way that preserves dollar hegemony depends critically on China, its largest creditor country. The increase in China's voting share in the World Bank from 2.7 percent to 4.4 percent (the US share remains at 16.4 percent) is an acknowledgement of this new geopolitical reality.

DANCING WITH THE DRAGON

In 2008 as the impact of the subprime crisis spiraled out into a global crisis, the Chinese government hardened the peg, keeping it firm at 6.8 renminbi to the dollar, in order to stave off the spillover from the unwinding of the financial markets. Despite the initial impact of slowdown in trade with the Great Recession, this policy and an aggressive stimulus policy have seen China weather the storm and emerge in 2010 with a projected growth rate of 9 percent and an IMF forecast for 2011 of nearly 10 percent. Accumulating about US$400 billion in reserves in 2009, the reserve holdings of China grew to US$2.4 trillion in January 2010.

China with its huge surplus and relatively buoyant economy is increasingly being viewed as an emerging challenge to the US. The diplomatic waltzes around the currency issue reflect the awkward balance of the dominant power and an upstart contender. The US has to appear to be coming down hard on China its leading creditor, and China has to appear not to be bowing down under pressure. The fact of the matter is that neither the US nor China is ready to rock the boat. After the escalation of tensions in spring 2010, there has been a lull. The US toned down the rhetoric on the currency issue and refrained from labeling China as a currency manipulator and the Chinese government sent out signals that it would allow its currency to appreciate, though at a time dictated by domestic considerations, not US interests. The prompt dispelling of rumors that China was moving out of the euro following the plunge in the currency (like its earlier statements regarding its continued commitment to investing in US treasury bills) suggest that China is invested in the stability of the global financial system. Its actions, specifically its currency interventions, as in the past during the Asian crisis, certainly have been integral to putting a back-stop to the international domino effect of financial crisis.

As long as China continues to maintain its capital controls and the limited convertibility of the renminbi, China cannot pose a real challenge to the dollar. There are, however, some signs that China is slowly fostering Yuan liquidity as a prelude to developing a more international role for the renminbi. The Chinese Central Bank has set up bilateral swap lines, independent of the IMF, amounting to a total of US$95 billion with Argentina, South Korea, Hong Kong, Indonesia, Belarus, and Malaysia broadening access to the renminbi. It has signed a deal with Brazil to increase the use of local currencies instead of dollars and another with Venezuela offering financial support, half of which will be paid in renminbi.[32]

After the fiasco of Chinese state-owned oil company China National Offshore Oil Corporation's (CNOOC's) attempt to acquire Unocal in 2005, China's US equity portfolio holdings have increased from US$4 billion in 2006 to US$93 billion in early 2010. Chinese financial investments were avidly sought after by US banks including Citibank and Merrill Lynch for the desperately needed injections of funds as the subprime crisis unfolded. In fact in 2009, Chinese acquisitions of US equity stakes surpassed US acquisitions of Chinese equity stakes for the first time.[33] At the same time four public sector Chinese banks have emerged in the top four slots in the ranking of financial institutions by the ratio of their share price to book value (the fifth is a Brazilian bank)! In 2000, US banks had occupied four of the top five slots.[34] While this does not necessarily suggest an eclipse of the global domination of US banks by Chinese state-owned financial institutions, the growing scale of these banks does point to a growing presence of China in global financial markets, and more importantly, the growing interpenetration of the relatively insulated Chinese banking structure with the US-dominated global financial system. Western banks, including J.P. Morgan and Citigroup, have begun promoting the use of the renminbi to settle trade with China.[35]

China has also been developing deeper economic relations with South East Asia, Africa, Brazil, and India (which accounted in the first 10 months of 2009 for 17.5 percent of China's trade compared with the US share of 13.5 percent).[36] These contrast sharply with the slowdown of trade with the US and Europe. China has displaced the US as the third largest trading partner of the ASEAN bloc. A Free Trade area—China–Asia Free Trade Area—with the ASEAN countries has come into effect in January 2010. Multilateral swap lines of US$120 billion have been set up under the Chiang Mai initiative. This initiative (an alternative regionally anchored rescue and financing mechanism) that was set in motion after the US Treasury and the IMF scuttled the proposal to set up an Asian Monetary Fund in the aftermath of the Asian crisis has further consolidated China's position in the region. Apart from forging deeper trade ties, China is also establishing stronger financial and investment ties in the region. Tensions have also been emerging with increased muscle flexing by China to assert its claims in the disputed islands in the South China Sea.

However, the accumulating surpluses in China are stoking the rapid growth in lending and credit creation. The US$500 billion stimulus launched by the Chinese state in response to the Great

Recession has been routed through loans issued by state-owned banks, further boosting the surge in credit. Bank loans doubled between 2008 and 2009, when new loans amounted to about one-third of China's GDP.[37] This credit bonanza has promoted a massive increase in investment, including investment in infrastructure and heavy industry. In 2009, fixed investment accounted for a whopping 47 percent of GDP.[38] With nearly half of GDP being channeled into fixed investment, the fears of overinvestment are very real. More importantly, this credit binge has fostered a boom in commercial and residential property. The exhaustion of this source of demand would abort the incipient recovery in developing countries.

At the same time a narrative of the rising dragon is marred by the steady flow of stories of appalling labor practices associated with high profile corporations. The news of the suicides by nine workers of Foxconn's factory at Shenzen in southern China where trendy electronic gizmos like iPads and iPhones are manufactured is the latest breach in the shiny façade of ascendant China.[39] The path forward remains to be seen. It might be a good time to question the regime of dollar hegemony that this uneasy embrace of the US and China represents.

Chapter 8

Beyond the Crisis

You never want a serious crisis to go to waste.

— Rahm Emmanuel, Chief of Staff at a Wall Street Journal Conference, November 21, 2008

The "authorized" account of the downturn that officially began in December 2007 dates the recession as having ended on June 2009, but it is clear that the US economy is still not out of the woods. Job creation remains sluggish and investment has not picked up pace, even though bank earnings have recovered. The top 1 percent of income earners captured 93 percent of the income gains in the first year of recovery.[1] The crisis has spilled over to the periphery of Europe, morphing into a sovereign debt crisis that has brought the Eurozone to the brink of break up. Emerging markets are finding their economies overheating with a flood of hot money. The fragile consensus that the states had to pull together in a coordinated strategy to revive the global economy and regulate finance is threatening to give way to a relapse toward protectionist "currency wars" and "beggar thy neighbor policies." No consensus has been reached yet on a levy on financial institutions or the appropriate standards for a capital buffer to protect banks from an unforeseen erosion of asset value. The initial embrace of concerted fiscal stimulus to pump-prime the flagging economy is now facing the chill of the fear of rising public debt and state spending.

Financial and corporate capital have launched the battle to restore their dominance. Is the Crisis going to waste?

This notion of crisis as an opportunity for social change is of course not a new notion. It was central to Karl Marx's notion that "crises are always but momentary and forcible solutions of the existing contradictions." Milton Friedman, a leading proponent of the neoliberal worldview, had written:

Only a crisis—actual or perceived—produces real change. When that crisis occurs, the actions that are taken depend on the ideas that are lying around. That, I believe, is our basic function: to develop alternatives to existing policies, to keep them alive and available until the politically impossible becomes the politically inevitable.[2]

In fact, the crisis of the 1970s had provided Friedman and his followers in the Chicago School with the opening to launch an attack on the prevailing Keynesian paradigm and seize the opportunity to push for the rollback of the developmental and welfare state in the Southern Cone of Latin America (starting with Chile under Pinochet) in the 1970s, and the UK and the US in the 1980s.[3]

The crisis of the "Golden Age of Capitalism" set the stage for the coup of finance and the consolidation of the hegemony of the dollar globally. The roots of this dominance of finance lie in the broader economic structure that was fashioned in the wake of the crisis, in particular the engineering of a broad realignment of forces and state power to squeeze workers' earnings while reorganizing work in a way that pushed the limits of worker productivity. The financial–managerial revolution fostered an extreme concentration of wealth in the US. Consumption demand came to be sustained by stoking private debt and asset bubbles. At the same time, the earnings of managers and executives became increasingly dependent on short-term returns, without having to bear the burden of the associated risk of long-term losses. The siphoning of surpluses to executive earnings also had implications for investment in productive capacity and savings in the US.

As production was relocated overseas, the US trade deficit began to rise and the US consumption demand became the locomotive driving global accumulation and the meteoric rise of China in particular. Emerging economies got increasingly integrated with the global network of production and financial flows dominated by US financial and corporate capital. The structural transformation of the US through the 1980s and 1990s was thus the foundation of the problem of global imbalances. The emergence of a "savings glut" in the developing world simply mirrors this process. Dollar hegemony was the pivot that sustained this mechanism of recycling surpluses from the rest of the world and the US's role as a banker to the world was buttressed by the ability to ward-off a speculative attack on its currency by exporting fragility to the periphery.

Does the crisis presage the demise of dollar hegemony? Does it herald the fall from grace of the "Washington Consensus" and the reign of the neoliberalism? Does it mark a shift in the balance of forces that established the growing power of finance and the consequent concentration of incomes in the hands of corporate and financial capital? If not, what are the prospects for a neoliberal reassertion being able to refire the engines of accumulation?

The current crisis reflects the tensions and contradictions of the global economy that was forged in the wake of the neoliberal revolution. It does in that sense provide an opening for initiating a process of structural change. The outcome is, however, not one that is preordained. The balance of forces can move in different ways.

185

The crisis has brought the vulnerabilities of the dollar standard into sharp relief. The governor of the People's Bank of China, Zhou Xiaochuan, in a much publicized speech, pointed to the urgent need to move beyond the volatile dollar standard toward an international reserve currency based on a basket of currencies that would be less susceptible to the priorities and agenda of a powerful state.[4] A UN panel of experts on the reform of the international monetary system also placed on the table a proposal for a new global reserve, based on an expanded SDR, as a means of addressing the contradictions of a single currency reserve system that fostered the export of fragility to the periphery and the appropriation of surpluses from the rest of world with growing global imbalances.[5] The proposal of the UN panel and that of the chairman of the People's Bank of China both draw on the Keynes Plan—the proposal that Keynes put forward during the Bretton Woods negotiations. The Keynes Plan sought to impart greater elasticity to the global economy by substituting a supranational credit mechanism in place of the gold standard, so that trade would not be limited by the access to gold, and countries would be able to adjust to persistent deficits without stalling growth and employment generation in their economics. At the same time such a mechanism would be better able to transcend the political constraints of a dominant key currency country. China and other surplus countries continue to diversify their holdings and have even stepped up central bank purchases of gold, but the initial momentum for the overhaul of the global financial system has receded. The euro crisis has left the dollar's hegemony without a credible challenge, at least for now. From the business press it is clear that both markets and corporations are factoring in the prospect of a breakup of the euro. The crisis, however, has not yet turned into a transformation of the dollar standard.

Meanwhile, the US states' continued reliance on monetary stimulus and successive forms of "quantitative easing" to get the economy out of its protracted stagnation has generated a mountain of public debt. While this policy has not had a significant impact on restoring investment domestically, funds in search of higher returns flooded the more buoyant emerging markets. In anticipation of a weakening of the dollar with further easing of lending by the Federal Reserve, investors are using this cheap money to bet on emerging market currencies. Capital flows to emerging market countries rose from US$531 billion in 2009 to US$1,088 billion in 2010.[6] This influx of hot money into emerging market economies prompted defensive policy measures to nip incipient speculative bubbles.

Capital controls, advocated by Keynes in his proposals for the Bretton Woods Conference, are once again finding a place in the policy arsenal of developing countries after decades of being discredited and taboo under the IMF–World Bank debt conditionality agreements. Such controls have been critical in the relative immunity that China and India in particular enjoyed from the most debilitating impacts of the financial meltdown. Brazil raised the tax on foreign investment in fixed income bonds, Korea launched audits of lenders dabbling in foreign currency derivatives, and Thailand has imposed a withholding tax on capital gains and interest payments on foreign bond holders. Central banks in emerging markets are being forced to intervene in the foreign exchange markets and buying US treasury securities in order to curb the appreciation of their currencies. Currency interventions by countries facing speculative inflows in effect help to mop up this glut of US treasuries, so that interest rates remain low despite the outflow of capital from the US. The US continues to enjoy its access to global surpluses, but the threat of debilitating currency wars is casting its shadow over the global economy.

187

The global economy's slide toward currency conflicts is thus a direct outcome of the concerted manner in which the Federal Reserve is stoking the fires of cheap credit. The swelling tide of public debt also means that the US agenda of refashioning the post-crisis world in a way that preserves dollar hegemony and the dominance of finance depends critically on China, its largest creditor. China, with its huge surplus and relatively buoyant economy, is increasingly being viewed as an emerging power that poses a challenge to the US.

China's intransigence, in not letting the renminbi appreciate, has become the favorite whipping horse in the narrative of the failure of multilateralism. The question is, however, not simply about exchange rates, but of income distribution and the asymmetry imposed by the dominance of finance and the dollar globally. So, inequality in the US becomes fodder for debt-fueled consumption, but in China with its different demographic and the conflicted virtue of having to accumulate its surpluses in dollars, low wages, and rising inequality has curbed consumption. The recent strike in a Honda transmission factory in Foshan (southern China) which led to the suspension of work in four Honda assembly plants in the region has had ripple effects as workers in other factories have begun to demand higher wages.[7] These worker actions and the redistribution of incomes in favor of workers in China rather than the appreciation of the Renminbi might provide the real impetus for rebalancing the global economy.

The diplomatic brouhaha around the currency issue reflects the awkward balance of a dominant power and an upstart contender. An analogy can be drawn with the destabilizing currency wars during the interwar period, when the US held the surpluses and was the emerging challenger to the hegemony of the UK. The Bretton Woods conference laid the ground for a cross-Atlantic coalition between the two powers that consolidated the dollar standard. The rise of the Group of 2—what has been christened Chimerica[8]—represents a far more uneasy coalition. China and the US continue to be locked in a balance of financial terror. China, despite its growing economic strength, remains for the time being subordinate to structures of finance dominated by US capital. Whether, and to what extent, the sovereign wealth funds and state-owned banks temper the norms and practices of private finance, or themselves become subsumed in their speculative logic remains to be seen.

Unlike the postwar period when the mechanisms of global coordination depended on a smaller group of advanced capitalist countries, the current crisis has thrown the more motley grouping of the G-20 countries to the fore. This reflects the changing geopolitical balance and the growing importance of not just China but also Brazil, Russia, India, and South Africa. Today, global negotiations face the formidable challenge of welding more disparate priorities, but at the same time offer an opening for more equitable and just global relations and a possible undermining of the political structures sustaining dollar hegemony.

The Bretton Woods institutions have been an integral element of this structure. Ever since the Asian crisis in 1997–98, countries bruised by the brutal deflationary regimens that the IMF conditionalities enforced became leery of IMF-coercive interventions. The IMF has also so far remained unsuccessful in its attempt to craft coordinated global rebalancing despite growing concerns over global imbalances over the past decade. As the crisis engulfed countries around the globe and in the periphery of Europe in particular, the role of the IMF is being redefined.

The scale of the crisis has prompted moves to triple the resources available to the IMF to US$750 billion to enable it to play a greater role. The IMF is now poised to boost its resources further to US$1 trillion. The fund has embarked on an overhaul of its lending framework. What the overhaul amounts to is a two-tier lending framework. On the one hand, there is the "no string loans" that works a bit like a precautionary insurance facility—for "strong performers" such as Mexico, Peru, Chile, Brazil, Singapore, South Korea, and Taiwan. On the other hand, conditionalities would continue to be imposed on countries with weaker "fundamentals" that do not yet meet this neoliberal yardstick, and progress in implementing "structural measures" still remains critical to keeping the program on track.

The relaxation of conditionality for the group of countries that meet this neoliberal yardstick for sound fundamentals is an acknowledgement of their changed status and the pressure to bring the stronger emerging economies into the mechanisms of global governance. The emergence of the Group of 20 (G-20) as the favored multilateral forum for coordinating strategies to manage the global economy reflects these same geopolitical imperatives. As the Anglo-Saxon model of financial capitalism is falling into disrepute, the political leaders in developing countries have acquired a handle to negotiate a more democratic restructuring of the international financial system. At the same time the seat at the high table of global governance that the US heads is also part of the complex diplomatic maneuvers to absorb these developing countries into the structures of dollar hegemony and to diffuse the potential challenge of China.

As the IMF seeks to quadruple its resources with additional contributions not only from the EU, Japan, and the US but also from China, Russia, Brazil, and India, a debate on the structure of the IMF, in particular the concentration of voting rights with the US and Europe, has been initiated. A transfer of about 5 percent of the quota shares (which also determine voting rights) from the advanced capitalist countries to stronger emerging economies is underway. This transfer comes largely at the expense of Europe, and leaves the US, which garners about 17 percent of the votes with its veto power over fund policy intact. There is also a parallel move to get European countries to give up at least two seats on the IMF board. The reforms would thus chip away at some of the clout of European countries, but would not compel the US to relinquish its overwhelming influence on the fund. However, the transfer of voting shares could give China, Brazil, India, and Russia the potential power to jointly shape the agenda of the fund. The bigger question is whether this could possibly be the brake that slows the neoliberal juggernaut.

The flawed understanding of how markets function lay at the heart of the neoliberal economic policy prescriptions. This flawed understanding contributed to the drive toward financial deregulation globally and has been the basis for the package of structural reforms that the IMF espouses while lending to developing countries. The revamp of the lending framework of the IMF does not suggest a real departure from the neoliberal paradigm responsible for the asymmetric assimilation of these countries into the international financial system. The criteria for the purposes of assessing qualifications for the "privilege" of a no-string loan in the two-tier framework arrangement include "a capital account position dominated by private flows and a track record of steady sovereign access to international capital markets at favorable terms." There are, however, some signs that the IMF is relenting in its orthodoxy on capital controls and its preoccupation with inflation targeting. A crucial obstacle is the design and implementation of coordinated capital controls that keep pace with financial innovations. Finance evolves new strategies in response to controls and regulations.

Clipping the wings of finance requires not just regulation but also a concerted containment of its power.

At the peak of the credit crunch, there was a remarkable revival of support for the idea of state intervention to restore the stalled economy. After three decades of banishment from the policy debate, the Keynesian policy prescription of a fiscal stimulus to revive private investment and growth acquired respectability in the dominant discourse. The collapse of demand in the wake of the Crash led to a cutback of investment and lending. The failure of the Federal Reserve policy of pumping liquidity through the policies of easing credit by soaking up assets from the jittery markets to revive investor confidence is a validation of Keynes's insights into the limits of monetary policy.

As the financial crisis metastasized into a sovereign debt crisis in Europe, the fragile consensus for fiscal stimulus began to fray as rising debt burdens and interest rates on the bonds of Greece, Spain, Italy, and Portugal, in particular, stoked fears of debt default. This transformation is not anomalous but follows the historical pattern.[9] As mounting sovereign debt burdens have set the stage for the revival of deficit vigilantes, the resolve for some sort of global stimulus pact to revive and regulate accumulation wavered. The G-20 meeting at Toronto in June 2010 came out with a proposal to reduce debt and slash budget deficits by half by 2013 and curb the growth of public debt. Across Europe, from Estonia to Germany and France, government spending is being brutally rolled back, with cuts in welfare spending, a rise in the retirement age, and retrenchment in the public sector. Britain announced the most drastic cuts in spending (of nearly 20 percent) in its postwar history in October 2010. Despite the slow recovery and the prospect of another recession, corporate and financial interests are clamoring for a cap on public debt and public spending.

The driving force in this backlash against state spending is a resurgent finance lobby. The underlying structure of power and inequality that had formed the basis of the neoliberal phase remains firmly entrenched in the aftermath of the crisis. The advanced capitalist countries remain mired in what could turn out to be a long stagnation and fiscal cutbacks are eroding the livelihoods and standards of living of large sections of the population, even as the banks are bouncing back. The widening social rift that growing inequality is fostering is spilling over in the form of swelling social tensions.

A groundswell of opposition has been growing in Europe. In Greece and Spain, in particular, widespread strikes, protests, and occupations signal that battle lines have been drawn. In France, school students joined workers in barricading the streets to protest against the pension reforms. Students in the UK marched on the streets and occupied the conservative party headquarters to oppose cuts on education spending. Popular resistance to austerity measures has also precipitated an early election. The Netherlands, with the Socialist Party, gained significant ground in the run up to the polls. Right wing, anti-immigrant, nationalist sentiment have also been resurgent as seen in the growing support for the Party for Freedom in the Netherlands, the British National Party in the UK, or the National Front in France. At stake in all these developments is refashioning of the neoliberal basis of the Euro-edifice. The primary concern of rescue efforts of the European Central Bank along with the European Commission and the IMF has been to restore the fortunes of banks and financial institutions (fortunes that were battered through their own reckless excesses) by privatizing social wealth. The core contradiction at the heart of the euro remains unresolved. In fact the clampdown on welfare spending, wages, and collective bargaining rights makes it even harder to sustain the euro. And yet any path toward a fundamental restructuring of the social basis of the euro is being thwarted by the dominant financial corporate oligarchy.

The US too is going into its presidential elections amidst a bitterly divisive campaign against government spending going amok. The bank bail outs, the stimulus plan, and the ongoing drain of the military adventures in Afghanistan and Iraq have led to a huge buildup of public debt. The management of this public debt is of imperative importance to the unfolding outcome of the global crisis, but it also holds the actions of the US State hostage to finance and further cements the Dollar-Wall Street nexus. So while the axe falls on public spending, infrastructure and job creation, and the fate of the health reform act and the social security structure is held ransom to fears of escalating budget deficits, the favored strategy to restore the economy is the policy of shoveling cheap money into the hands of finance and corporate capital in the hope that investment will pick up pace. Instead, this cheap money has helped capital markets recover and the earnings of finance gather steam by moving into the more lucrative emerging market economies. It is not clear, however, whether these myopic strategies to boost the earnings of finance could form a sustainable basis of accumulation.

Capital markets do appear to have recovered faster than labor or housing markets. After shaking off the heat and dust of public outrage at the banker's hubris and greed, the banks are back to business as usual. To give an example, securities lending, where clients commission a bank to lend its financial assets to another investor in return for cash that is invested by the same banks in further trades, has rebounded sharply. If the trade goes sour, the client bears the losses but the banks can claim as much as 40 percent of any gains! This revival of securities lending provides a rich fodder to speculative trading. By September 2010 shares worth US\$2.3 trillion had been loaned out, an amount that was nearly back to its pre-Crash level of US\$2.5 trillion in 2007.[10]

The recent disclosure of the slipshod and error-ridden methods, including fudging and "robo-signing" documents that banks pursued in their rush to foreclose homes in the wake of the crisis had forced banks including Bank of America and JPMorgan Chase call a temporary halt to foreclosures. The reluctance of the US government to impose a longer term moratorium on foreclosures that might jeopardize the resumption of bank earning, while keeping out-of-work families in their homes, is a sign of how implicated the state is in the power structure of the reign of finance. This is seen again in the US\$26 billion settlement reached in February 2012, with five major mortgage servicers including Bank of America and Citibank which grants them a waiver from federal prosecution provided by the settlement, protecting them from billions of dollars worth of lawsuits.

It has also come to light that major banks including JPMorgan Chase, Bank of America, UBS, Lehman Brothers, and Bear Stearns have conspired and colluded to deliberately rig the public bids on municipal bonds, a business worth about US\$3.7 trillion.[11] By skimming tiny fractions of percentages off the rates on these multi-million dollar bids, the banks have been siphoning off huge sums from the all ready cash-strapped municipalities across the US.[12] For this subversion of government contracts, the Bank of America got away with a paltry fine of US\$137 million while JPMorgan Chase shelled out US\$228 million, while continuing to enjoy the "privilege" of managing municipal business! These scandals are a symptom of the deeper fault lines in the structure of the US economy. These fault lines have to do with the asymmetry that allows the big banks to be absolved of the consequences of their reckless and predatory trades, while working class households that were sucked into the vortex of debt were not granted the same latitude. In the same way, Goldman Sachs has escaped prosecution for deliberately defrauding clients by selling them pools of dodgy mortgages while betting against them, getting away with a settlement of US$550 million. An entire arsenal of lobbying power has also been deployed to thwart any regulatory pushback to this plunder.

The irony is that the neoliberal rhetoric of free markets that is deployed to justify obscene levels of profiteering and to deter any forms of regulation is promoting a financial system where markets and market discipline have been banished. It is bad enough that in the world of exotic custom-built financial products and over-the-counter derivatives, the "models" spawned by the industry have completely usurped the role of the "market" that economic theory celebrates. We now know that these models, which proxy for the market, have been built around a fictional price—the LIBOR—where no real market exists. The LIBOR is the rate at which leading banks can borrow from each other in the London markets and also more critically the anchor of about US$800 trillion worth of international financial transactions.[13] The disclosure that traders associated with major banks including Barclays, Bank of America, JPMorgan Chase, and Citibank colluded to manipulate these pivotal LIBOR rates has exposed the hollow core of the financial markets. While vociferously maintaining that self-regulation and unregulated market forces were the most effective form of discipline, the financial oligarchy has established its monopolistic stranglehold right at the heart of the ballooning international financial system. Not only has regulatory control been preempted and criminal prosecution been avoided

196

but the financial oligarchy has also sought for itself immunity from market discipline!

The US state has been caught up in the need to bail out large banks and balks at touching the earnings of the executives, but the contracts guaranteeing pensions and benefits to ordinary workers is not viewed favorably. There has been unrelenting pressure to dismantle worker protection and bargaining power, and tighten predatory grip of debt on poorer households. Perversely, even as workers in the private sector continue to be squeezed in the face of tepid job growth, and are forced to accept pay cuts when they return to work, public sector workers are emerging as a target of the neoliberal backlash after the wreckage of the crisis. The concessions forced on the autoworkers, including the recent acceptance of a two-tiered structure that grants new workers lower levels of pay and benefits as the price of expanding jobs signaled an attack on the last remaining bastion of the middle class blue-collar worker of the golden age of US capitalism. The assault has turned to the benefits that public sector employees continue to enjoy despite three decades of the erosion of working class power with the growing power of finance. In the cross-fire are a range of public sector workers from teachers to fire-fighters and postal workers. And so, once the worst of the panic was over and the "official" recovery was underway, pieces began to appear in the business press decrying the "government pay boom" and the widening divide between public sector and private sector workers, and the public sector employee being portrayed as the dominant "elite," the privileged class whose "disproportionate" benefits are being drawn from the earnings of the tax payer.[14]

With the erupting fiscal crisis of states and local governments in the US, this major source of employment in the US is drying up. By July 2012, budget cuts at the state and local levels have led to a shedding of about 627,000 public sector jobs since June 2009.[15] These budget crises, further intensified by sops and concessions given to business, have become the basis on which a deliberate assault on collective bargaining rights has been launched. In the spring of 2011, the recently elected Governor of Wisconsin, Scott Walker, rammed through a bill that would not simply cut wages and benefits wages but also sharply curtail the collective bargaining rights of public sector unions. This emergency measure in the wake of the fiscal crisis came right after his government had passed a legislation that handed out about US$117 million in tax breaks to corporations.[16] This move sparked a long and heroic siege of the state capital as protestors came out in huge numbers. Similar assaults on collective bargaining rights were also initiated in the states of Ohio, Tennessee, and Indiana, triggering protests.

By the fall of 2011, the outrage against these resistances had erupted into the widespread "Occupy" protests across the US. The slogan of the "Occupy Wall Street" movement—"We are the 99 percent"—captures this sense of outrage at the growing concentration of power in the hands of an elite coterie and the widening chasm that separates this elite from the rest of the American people. It also expresses a popular perception that the excesses and hubris of the richest 1 percent of US households that had brought on the protracted crisis of the global economy have not been contained. With this movement the spotlight was turned on the distributional and structural basis of the crisis.

Given the interpenetration of the power of the state and that of financial and corporate capital, it is not surprising that a lot of the public outrage, in the face of deepening inequality and persistent joblessness in the US has been directed against the state. Some of this rage is in effect being harnessed and deployed by corporate and financial interests to further their own agenda. Billionaires like the Koch Brothers who head an oil and energy conglomerate and Rupert Murdoch who controls the powerful Fox media group have pumped millions of dollars to such campaigns.[17] The powerful hold of corporate power has been evident in the dilution and continued pressure to rollback healthcare reform, resistance to letting the Bush era tax cuts to the top income brackets expire, the gridlock over the jobs bill or the debt ceiling. With the recent Supreme Court ruling, in the Citizen's United versus the Federal Election Commission case, overthrowing the ban on corporate spending during elections, the stage has been set for the exercise of corporate power even more blatantly and pervasively. With a deluge of uncapped donations pouring in from the corporate elites, the super PACS—the "outside" political groups ostensibly unrelated to a particular candidate—spent nearly US$280 million since the start of the US presidential campaign by September 30. Both the Democratic and the Republican presidential campaigns have spent more than 600 million each on this election, which promises to be the most expensive election in US history.[18] Corporate-backed money power has been unleashed on an unprecedented scale to shape and subvert the electoral process.

Which is not to say that this crisis is an opportunity that has already been lost for those hoping for a more sane and equitable restructuring of the economy and some amelioration of the corrosive impact of deep and growing inequality on the lives of ordinary working households and on society. Signs of outrage are evident across the globe—in the uprisings against dictatorial regimes in Tunisia, Egypt, Libya, and other countries in the Middle East; in the strikes in Greece, the demonstrations of the *indignados* in Spain and the militant protests in Italy as fiscal cutbacks destroy jobs and social cushions; and in the groundswell of the "Occupy Wall Street" movement in the US. There is a common chord that connects these diverse expressions of popular unrest. In different ways, and to different degrees, these revolts reflect the frustration and anger of ordinary people around the world, who feel increasingly marginalized by an accumulation paradigm that has allowed a small globally connected elite to corner the gains of economic growth. Four years after the collapse of Lehman, as we contemplate the first anniversary of the Occupy protests, it is clear that shaking off the pervasive hold of finance on state structure and on ordinary lives across the globe is not going to be easy.

Notes and References

CHAPTER 1

1. J.K. Galbraith, *The Great Crash of 1929* (Boston: Houghton Mifflin Company, 1997).
2. Lisa Endlich, *Goldman Sachs: The Culture of Success* (New York: Simon & Shuster, 2000).
3. Galbraith, *The Great Crash of 1929*.
4. Galbraith, *The Great Crash of 1929*.
5. Endlich, *Goldman Sachs*, 47.
6. Galbraith, *The Great Crash of 1929*.
7. L. Robbins, *The Great Depression* (New York: Macmillan, 1934).
8. C. Kindleberger, *Manias Panics and Crashes: A History of Financial Crisis* (New York: Macmillan, 1989).
9. S. Keen, "Finance and Economic Breakdown: Modeling Minsky's Financial Instability Hypothesis," *Journal of Post Keynesian Economics*, 17(4, 1995).
10. Galbraith, *The Great Crash of 1929*, 15.
11. D. Colander, H. Follmer, A. Haas, M. Goldberg, K. Juselius, A. Kirman, T. Lux, and B. Sloth, "The Financial Crisis and the Systematic Failure of Academic Economists," *Dahlem Workshop* (2005); P. Krugman, "How Did Economists Get It so Wrong," *New York Times*, September 2, 2008.
12. T. Besley and P. Henessy, "Letter to the Queen of England." http://media.ft.com/cms/3e3b6ca8-7a08-11de-b86f-00144feabdc0pdf.
13. D.J. Bezemer, "No One Saw This Coming: Understanding Financial Crisis through Accounting Models" (Munich Personal RePec Archive Paper No. 15892, 2009).

14. S. Keen, "The Runaway Train of Debt," *DebtWatch*, November, 2006.

15. D. Baker, "The Run-Up in Home Prices: Is It Real or Is It Another Bubble?" *CEPR*, August, 2002. www.cepr.net/index.php/publications/reports; D. Baker, B. DeLong, and P. Krugman, "Asset Returns and Economic Growth," *Brookings Papers on Economic Activity*, p. 1, 2005.

16. W. Godley and G. Zezza, "Debt and Lending: A Cri de Coeur," *Policy Brief*, (Levy Institute of Economics), 2006.

17. Postings on the Roubini Global Economics Monitor (now Roubini Global Economics).

18. P. Krugman, "Running out of Bubbles," *New York Times*, May 27, 1999.

19. B. Eichengreen, "The Last Temptation of Risk," *The National Interest*, March, 2010; "Larry Summers and the Subversion of Economics," *Chronicle of Higher Education*, October 2010.

20. For instance, G. Dumenil and D. Levy, *The Crisis of Neoliberalism* (Cambridge: Harvard University Press, 2010); G. Albo, L. Panitch, and S. Gindin, *In and Out of Crisis: The Global Financial Meltdown and Left Alternatives* (P.M. Press, 2010); J.B. Foster and F. Magdoff, *The Great Financial Crisis: Causes and Consequences* (New York: Monthly Review Press, 2009); D. Harvey, *The Enigma of Capital and the Crisis of Capitalism* (Oxford: Oxford University Press, 2010).

CHAPTER 2

1. Leader, "The Financial Crisis: What Next," *Economist*, September 20, 2008.

2. The chronicle of the unfolding events presented in this chapter is drawn largely from contemporary newspaper reports, the *Financial Times*, the *New York Times*, the *Economist* and also from the A.R. Sorkin, *Too Big to Fail: The Inside Story of How Wall Street and Washington Fought to Save the Financial System from Crisis and Themselves* (New York: Viking Adult, 2009).

3. Geoffrey Elliot, *The Mystery of Overend and Gurney* (London: Methuen, 2006).

4. W. Cohan, *The House of Cards: A Tale of Hubris and Wretched Excess on Wall Street* (New York: Doubleday, 2009); Bryan Burrough, *Bringing down Bear Stearns* (Vanity Fair, 2008).

5. H.S. Shin, *Modern Bank Runs: A Case Study of Northern Rock*, 2008. http://www.princeton.edu/~hsshin/www/nr.pdf.

6. Burrough, *Bringing down Bear Stearns.*

7. G. Morgenson, "Behind the Countrywide Lending Spree," *New York Times*, August 26, 2007.

8. Morgenson. "Behind the Countrywide Lending Spree."

9. Burrough. *Bringing down Bear Stearns.*

10. Morgenson, "Behind the Countrywide Lending Spree."

11. New York Times, "L. Story Regulators Seize Mortgage Lender," *New York Times,* July 12, 2008.

12. F. Mosely, "The Bailout of Fannie Mae and Freddie Mac," in *The Economic Crisis Reader*, ed. G. Friedman, F. Moseley, and C. Sturr (Dollars and Sense, 2009).

13. A.R. Sorkin, "The Race to Save Lehman," *New York Times*, October 20, 2009.

14. H. Sender, F. Gurerrea, P.T. Laarsen, and G. Silverman, "Broken Brothers: How Brinkmanship was not Enough to Save Lehman," *Financial Times*, September 15, 2008.

15. Money Market, "Foreign Bondholders and not the US Money Market Drove the Fannie and Freddie Bail Out," *Money Market*, September 11, 2008. http://moneymorning.com/2008/09/11/fnm/.

16. J. Pollit, "Lender's Crisis is Paulson's big moment," *Financial Times*, August 24, 2008.

17. G. Morgenson, "How the Thundering Herd Faltered and Fell." *New York Times*, November 9, 2008.

18. T. Alloway, "BOA MER Due Diligence Trading Edition," *FT Alphaville*, March 6, 2009.

19. G. Morgenson, "Behind Insurers Crisis, Blind Eye to a Web of Risk," *New York Times*, September 27, 2008.

20. G. Morgenson, "Testy Conflict With Goldman Helped Push A.I.G. to Edge," *New York Times*, February 6, 2010.

21. G. Morgenson, "Behind Insurers Crisis, Blind Eye to a Web of Risk." *New York Times*, September 27, 2008.
22. G. Morgenson and L. Story, "Testy Conflict with Goldman Helped Push AIG to the Edge." *New York Times*, February 7, 2010.
23. T. Alloway, BOA MER due diligence trading edition, *FT Alphaville*, March 6, 2009.
24. Morgenson, "How the Thundering Herd Faltered and Fell."
25. Joe Nocera, "As the Credit Crisis Spiraled, Alarm Led to Action," *New York Times*, October 2, 2008.

CHAPTER 3

1. J. Gapper, "Last Gasp of the Broker Dealer," *Financial Times*, September 16, 2008.
2. G. Tett, *Fool's Gold: How the Bold Dream of a Small Tribe at J.P. Morgan Was Corrupted by Wall Street Greed and Unleashed a Catastrophe* (New York: Free Press, 2009).
3. P. Augar, "Do Not Exaggerate Investment Banking's Death," *Financial Times*, September 22, 2008.
4. T. Geithner, "Reducing Systemic Risk in a Dynamic Financial System" *Remarks at The Economic Club of New York*, 2008.
5. P. Gowan, "Crisis in the Heartland: Consequences of the New Wall Street System," *New Left Review*, 55 (2009).
6. H.S. Shin, "Securitization and Financial Stability," *Economic Journal*, 119 (2009): 309–32.
7. Shin, "Securitization and Financial Stability."
8. Tett, *Fool's Gold*.
9. Tett, *Fool's Gold*.
10. N. Shwarz and E. Dash, "Questions for Banks that Put Together Deals," *New York Times*, April 21, 2010.
11. G. Morgenson and L. Story, "Banks Bundled Bad Debt, Bet Against It and Won," *New York Times*, December 24, 2009.
12. D. Greenlaw, J. Hatzius, A.K. Kashyap, and H.S. Shin, "Leveraged Losses: Lessons from the Mortgage Market Meltdown," *US Monetary Policy*

Forum Report No. 2, Rosenberg Institute, Brandeis International Business School and Initiative on Global Markets, University of Chicago Graduate School of Business, 2008.

13. P. Mehrling, "The Global Credit Crisis and Policy Response, 2010," Remarks prepared for IRE and EPS Workshop, The Financial and Banking Crisis: Looking for Solutions, Paris, 2009.

14. J. Hamilton, "Borrowing Short and Lending Long," *Econbrowser*, September 6, 2007. http://www.econbrowser.com/archives/2007/09/borrowing_ short.html; C.A. Goodhart, "The Background to the 2007 Financial Crisis," *International Economics and Economic Policy*, 2007.

15. Geithner, "Reducing Systemic Risk in a Dynamic Financial System."

16. J. Kregel, "Minsky's Cushions of Safety: Systemic Risk and the Crisis in the US Subprime Mortgage Market," The Levy Institute of Bard College. *Public Policy Brief*, 93, 2008.

17. Mehrling, "The Global Credit Crisis and Policy Response, 2010."

18. Mehrling, "The Global Credit Crisis and Policy Response, 2010."

19. C.R. Morris, *The Trillion Dollar Meltdown: Easy Money, High Rollers and the Great Credit Crash* (New York: Public Affairs, 2008).

20. D. Baker, *Plunder and Blunder: The Rise and Fall of the Bubble Economy* (Sausalito, CA: Polipoint Press, 2009).

21. Baker, *Plunder and Blunder.*

22. D. Henwood, "Leaking Bubble," *Nation*, March, 2006.

23. L. Story, "Home Equity Frenzy Was a Bank Ad Come True," *New York Times*, August 15, 2008.

24. D. Henwood, "Crisis of a Gilded Age," *Nation*, September, 2008.

25. R. Blackburn, "The Subprime Crisis," *New Left Review*, 50 (2008).

26. Centre for Responsible Lending, *A Snapshot of the Subprime Market*, November 27, 2007. http://www.responsiblelending.org.

27. C.A.E.Goodhart, "Background to the 2007 Financial Crisis." *International Economics and Economic Policy*, 4 (4, 2008). http://link.springer.com/ journal/10368.

28. H. Minsky, *John Maynard Keynes* (New York: Columbia Press, 1975); H. Minsky, *Stabilizing an Unstable Economy* (McGraw Hill, 1986); H. Minsky, "Securitization. The Levy Economics Institute of Bard College," Policy Note, 2008.

29. K. Marx, *Capital Vol. I* (New York: Vintage Books, 1977), 235.

30. Marx, *Capital Vol. I*, 236.
31. Y. Smith, *Econned: How Unenlightened Self interest Undermined Democracy and Corrupted Capitalism* (New York: Palgrave-Macmillan, 2010); R. Rajan, "Has Financial Development Made the World Riskier?" Federal Reserve of Kansas City, 2005.
32. Ludwig Heinrich Edler von Mises, "Economic Calculation in the Socialist Commonwealth," in *Collectivist Economic Planning*, ed. Freidrich Von Hayek (London: Routledge and Kegan Paul, 1935).
33. D. Foley, "The Unresolved Moral Dilemmas of Contemporary Capitalism," lecture at Colorado State University, February, 2009; J. Stiglitz, *Freefall: America, Free Markets and the Sinking of the Global Economy* (New York: W.W. Norton, 2010).
34. D. Colander, H. Follmer, A. Haas, M. Goldberg, K. Juselius, A. Kirman, T. Lux, and B. Sloth, "The Financial Crisis and the Systematic Failure of Academic Economists," Dahlem Workshop, 2008; P. Krugman, "How Did Economists Get It so Wrong," *New York Times*, September 2, 2009; B. Eichengreen, "The Last Temptation of Risk," *The National Interest*, March 26, 2010.

CHAPTER 4

1. Ben S. Bernanke, "Deflation: Making Sure 'It' Doesn't Happen Here," Remarks before the National Economists Club. Washington, DC, 2002.
2. Martin Mayer, The Fed: The Inside Story of How the World's Most Powerful Financial Institution Drives the Market (New York: Free Press, 2001).
3. P. Goodman and L. Story, "Overseas Investors buy Aggressively in the US," *New York Times*, January 20, 2008.
4. George Stiglitz, "A Better Bail Out," *Nation*, September 26, 2008; Nouriel Roubini, "Is Purchasing $700 Billion of Toxic Assets the Best Way to Recapitalize the Financial System? No! It is Rather a Disgrace and Rip-Off Benefiting Only the Shareholders and Unsecured Creditors of Banks," September 28, 2008. www.rgemonitor.
5. Dealbook, "Asked about Shift Paulson Says 'Facts Changed'," *New York Times*, November 12, 2008.

6. G. Morgenson and L. Story, "It Inside the Bailout of AIG: Extra Forgive-ness for Big Banks," *New York Times*, August 12, 2010; G. Morgenson and L. Story, "Two at Fed Had Doubts over Payout to AIG," *New York Times*, January 26, 2010.

7. Congressional Oversight Panel. *Valuing Treasury's Acquisitions*, February 2009. http://cop.senate.gov/documents/cop-020609-report.pdf.

8. Center of Media and Democracy. *Real Economy Project*. http://www.sourcewatch.org/index.php?title=Total_Wall_Street_Bailout_Cost.

9. P. Mehrling, "The New Lombard Street: Anatomy of Crisis," paper present-ed at the Institute of New Economic Thought Conference, Kings College, 2010.

10. R. Vasudevan, "Credit Crisis: Is the International Role of the Dollar at Stake?" *Monthly Review*, 60 (11, April 2009).

11. Mehrling, "The New Lombard Street."

12. S. Jones, "If All Else Fails Devalue the Dollar," November 2009, *FT Al-phaville*. http://ftalphaville.ft.com/blog/2008/11/18/18355/if-all-else-fails-devalue-the-dollar/.

13. W. Buiter and A. Sibert, "The Central Bank as Market Maker of Last Resort." Voxeu, August 13, 2007. http://www.voxeu.org/index.php?q=node/459.

14. Mehrling, "The New Lombard Street."

15. Mehrling, "The New Lombard Street."

16. N. Roubini, "Helicopter Ben goes ZIRP and more while the global economy enters stag-deflation RGE Monitor." http://www.rgemonitor.com. Also see Martin Wolf, "Helicopter Ben' Confronts the Challenge of a Lifetime," *Financial Times*, December 16, 2008.

17. Vasudevan, "Credit Crisis."

18. Vasudevan, "Credit Crisis."

19. A. Haldane, "Banking on the State," *BIS Review*, 139 (2009).

20. Haldane, "Banking on the State."

21. G. Tett, *Fool's Gold: How the Bold Dream of a Small Tribe at J.P. Morgan was Corrupted by Wall Street Greed and Unleashed a Catastrophe* (New York: Free Press, 2009).

22. S. Johnson and J. Kwaak, *13 Bankers: The Wall Street Takeover and the Next Financial Meltdown* (New York: Pantheon Books, 2010), 180.

23. Johnson and Kwaak, *13 Bankers.*

24. M. King, "Speech to Scottish Business Organizations," *Edinburgh*, October 2009. http://www.bankofengland.co.uk/publications/speeches/2009/speech406.pdf.

25. L. Kotlikoff, *Jimmy Stewart Is Dead* (New Jersey: Wiley and Sons, 2010).

26. S. Keen, "Bailing out the Titanic with a Thimble," *Economic Analysis and Policy*, 39(1, 2009).

27. J. Stiglitz, *Freefall: America Free Markets and the Sinking of the World Economy* (New York: WW Norton and Company, 2010), 64.

28. J. Bernstein, "The Jobless Recovery," *Economic Policy Institute Policy Brief*, 2003, 186; R. Pollin, "Deepening Divides in the US Economy, Jobless Recovery and the Return of Fiscal Deficits," PERI Working Paper, 2004.

29. D. Autor, *The Polarization of Job Opportunities in the US Labor Market: Implications for Employment and Earnings*, Center for American Progress and The Hamilton Project, 2010.

30. Editorial, "As the Economy Slows," *New York Times*, August 8, 2010.

31. D. Leonhardt, "For Those with jobs, a Recession with Some Benefits," *New York Times*, August 10, 2010.

32. Keen. 2009. "Bailing out the Titanic with a Thimble."

33. H. Shierholz, "Fifteen Months since Recession's Official End," Economy Short 11.5 Million Jobs. Economic Policy Institute, October, 2010. http://www.epi.org/publications/entry/september_jobs_picture.

34. Bureau of Labor Statistics, "Job Openings and Labor Turnover Survey," February, 2010. http://data.bls.gov/cgi-bin/surveymost?jt.

35. L. Mishel, H. Shierholz, and K.A. Edwards, "Reasons for Skepticism about Structural Unemployment," Policy Institute Briefing Paper 279, 2010.

36. E. Dash and J. Healy, "Citigroup Sheds Energy Unit and Its $100 Million Trader," *New York Times*, October 9, 2009.

37. A.R. Sorkin, "A Bridge Loan The US should guide G.M. in a Chapter.11," *New York Times*, November 17, 2008.

38. L. Mishel, "Corporate Profits Have Recovered, but Job Market still Depressed," Economic Policy Institute, July 14, 2010.

39. R. Reich, "Time to Take Wall Street out of Washington," *Financial Times*, April 26, 2010.

40. S. Johnson and J. Kwaak, *13 Bankers*; N. Prins, *It Takes a Pillage: An Epic Tale of Power, Deceit and Untold Trillions* (New York: Wiley, 2010).

CHAPTER 5

1. G. Krippner, "Financialization of the US Economy," *Socio-Economic Review*, 23(2, 2005).
2. G. Duménil and D. Lévy, "The Crisis of Neoliberalism and US Hegemony," *Kurswechsel*, 2 (2009): 6–13. http://jourdan.ens.fr/levy/dle2009d.htm; G. Dumenil and D. Levy, *Capital Resurgent* (Cambridge: Harvard University Press, 2004).
3. J. Crotty, "If Financial Market Competition Is so Intense, Why Are Financial Firm Profits so High? Reflections on the Current 'Golden Age' of Finance," University of Massachusetts, Amherst: Political Economy Research Institute, Working Paper Series no. 134, 2007.
4. T. Phillippon and A. Resheff, "Wages and Human Capital in the US Banking Industry: 1909–2006," (NBER Working Paper 14644, 2009).
5. L. Mishel, J. Bernstein, and H. Shierholz, "State of Working America 2008–9," Economic Policy Institute.
6. Robin Blackburn, "Finance and the Fourth Dimension," *New Left Review* 39 (2006): 39–70.
7. T. Piketty and E. Saez, "Income and Wage Inequality in the US: 1913–2002," in *Top Incomes over the Twentieth Century*, edited by A.B. Atkinson and T. Piketty, 2007. http://elsa.berkeley.edu/~saez/piketty-saezOUP04US.pdf.
8. Piketty and Saez, "Income and Wage Inequality in the US."
9. A. Sherman, *Income Gaps Hit Record Levels. In 2006: New Data Show Rich-Poor Gap Tripled Between 1979 and 2006.* Center on Budget and Policy Priorities, 2009.
10. Piketty and Saez, "Income and Wage Inequality in the US."
11. Internal Revenue Service, "The 400 Individual Income Tax Returns Reporting the Highest Adjusted Gross Incomes each Year, 1992–2007."
12. L. Panitch and S. Gindin, "Finance and the American Empire," in *Socialist Register: The Empire Reloaded*, edited by Leo Panitch and Colin Leys. New York: Monthly Review Press, 2005.
13. K. Moody, *An Injury to All* (New York: Verso, 1988).
14. R. Brenner, "The Economics of Global Turbulence," *New Left Review*, 229 (1998).

209

15. A. Glyn, *Capitalism Unleashed* (London: Oxford University Press, 2006).

16. Glyn, *Capitalism Unleashed*.

17. C. Lapvitsas, "Financialized Capitalism: Crisis and Financial Expropriation," *Historical Materialism*, 17 (2, 2009); R. Blackburn, "The Sub Prime Crisis," *New Left Review*, 50 (2008).

18. US Federal Reserve. Survey of Consumer Finances. http://www.federalreserve.gov/pubs/oss/oss2/about.html.

19. J. Garcia, "Still Borrowing to Make Ends Meet," *Demos*, November, 2007.

20. J.B. Foster, *The Great Financial Crisis* (New York: Monthly Review Press, 2009).

21. S. Keen, "The Credit Tsunami," in *The Economic Crisis Reader*, G. Friedman, F. Moseley, and C. Sturr (eds). New York: Dollars and Sense, 2009.

22. Phillipon and Resheff, "Wages and Human Capital in the US Banking Industry."

23. Dumenil and Levy, *The Crisis of Neoliberalism*; D. Kotz, "The Financial and Economic Crisis of 2008: A Systemic Crisis of Neoliberal Capitalism," *Review of Radical Political Economy*, 41(3, 2009).

24. S. Mohun, "The Crisis of 2008 in Historical Perspective," May 2010, Table 4.

25. Kotz, "The Financial and Economic Crisis of 2008."

26. Mohun, "The Crisis of 2008 in Historical Perspective."

27. K. Moody, *Workers in a Lean World: Unions in the International Economy* (London: Verso).

28. Mohun, "The Crisis of 2008 in Historical Perspective."

29. Dumenil and Levy, *The Crisis of Neoliberalism*; Mohun, "The Crisis of 2008 in Historical Perspective."

30. Dumenil and Levy, *Capital Resurgent.*

31. G. Dumenil and D. Levy, *The Great Depression: A Paradoxical Event*, 1995. http://jourdan.ens.fr/levy/dle1995e.htm; Dumenil and Levy, *Capital Resurgent*; Dumenil and Levy, "The Crisis of Neoliberalism and US Hegemony"; Mohun, "The Crisis of 2008 in Historical Perspective."

32. G. Epstein and J. Schor, "The Federal Reserve Treasury Accord and the Construction of the Post war Monetary Regime," *Social Concept*, 7(1, 1994).

CHAPTER 6

1. GDF online.
2. BIS, Triennial Central Bank Survey, Foreign Exchange and Derivative market, Basel 2007; Gabriele Galati and Phillip Wooldridge, "The Euro as a Reserve Currency: A Challenge to the Pre-eminence of the US Dollar?" *BIS Working Papers*, 2006, 218.
3. R. Vasudevan, "From the Gold Standard to the Floating Dollar Standard: An Appraisal in the Light of Marx's Theory of Money," *Review of Radical Political Economy*, 41 (4, 2009): 473–91.
4. F.L. Block, *The Origins of International Economic Disorder: A Study of United States International Monetary Policy from World War II to the Present* (Berkeley: University of California Press, 1977); E. Helleiner, *States and the Reemergence of Global Finance: From Bretton Woods to the 1990s* (Ithaca: Cornell University Press, 1994).
5. Eric Helleiner, *States and the Reemergence of Global Finance: From Bretton Woods to the 1990s* (Ithaca: Cornell University Press, 1994).
6. James Boughton, "North West of Suez: The 1956 Crisis and the Suez," *IMF Staff Papers,* 48 (3, 2001): 425–46.
7. Leo Panitch and Sam Gindin, "Finance and the American Empire," *Socialist Register: The Empire Reloaded* (Monmouth: Merlin Press, 2005).
8. R. Parboni, *The Dollar and Its Rivals* (New York: Verso, 1985).
9. E. Dickens, "The Eurodollar Market and the New Era of Financialization," in *Financialization and the World Economy*, edited by G. Epstein, 210–19. Northampton, MA: Edward Elgar, 2005.
10. Helleiner, *States and the Reemergence of Global Finance.*
11. Dickens, "The Eurodollar Market and the New Era of Financialization,"; Helleiner, *States and the Reemergence of Global Finance.*
12. David E. Spiro, *The Hidden Hand of American Hegemony* (Ithaca: Cornell University Press, 1999).
13. Helleiner, *States and the Reemergence of Global Finance.*
14. Blaise Gadanecz, "The Syndicated Loan Market: Structure, Development and Implications," *BIS Quarterly Review*, December, 2004, 75–89.
15. Global Development Finance.

16. J. Kregel, "Derivatives and Global Capital Flows: Applications to Asia," *Cambridge Journal of Economics*, 22 (1998): 677–76.

17. R. Dodd, "The Role of Derivatives in the East Asian Financial Crisis," in *International Capital Markets: Systems in Transition*, edited by J. Eatwell and L. Taylor, 447–74. Oxford and New York: Oxford University Press, 2002.

18. BIS, Triennial Central Bank Survey, 2007.

19. Dodd, "The Role of Derivatives in the East Asian Financial Crisis."

20. J. Crotty and K. Lee, "Neo Liberal Restructuring in Post Crisis Korea," in *Financialization and the World Economy*, edited by G. Epstein. Northampton, MA: Edward Elgar, 2005.

21. R. Vasudevan, "Dollar Hegemony, Financialization and the Credit Crisis," *Review of Radical Political Economics*, 41(3, 2009): 291–304.

22. R. Vasudevan, "Finance Imperialism and the Hegemony of the Dollar," *Monthly Review*, April, 2008.

23. M. Bordo and B. Eichengreen, "Crises Now and Then: What Lessons from the Last Era of Financial Globalization," National Bureau of Economic Research, Inc. NBER Working Papers 8716, 2002.

24. M. Wolf, *Fixing Global Finance* (Baltimore: John Hopkins Press, 2008), 31.

25. M. Dooley, D. Folkerts-Landau, and P. Graber, "The Revived Bretton Woods System," *International Journal of Finance and Economics,* 9(4, 2004): 307–13.

26. R. Brenner, *The Boom and the Bubble: The US in the World Economy* (London: W.W. Norton, 2002).

27. N. Fergusson, "The End of Chimerica: Amiable Divorce or Currency War, Testimony before US House of Representatives committee on Ways and Means," 2002. http://waysandmeans.house.gov/media/pdf/111/10-03-24_Ferguson_Testimony.pdf.

28. Nouriel Roubini, "US-China Currency and Trade Collision Course," *Roubini Global Economics*, February, 24.

29. P. Gourinchas and H. Rey, "From World Banker to World Venture Capitalist: US External Adjustment and the Exorbitant Privilege," *NBER Working Paper 11563*. National Bureau of Economic Research, Cambridge, MA, 2005.

30. G. Dumenil and D. Levy, "Thirty Years of Neoliberalism under US Hegemony," in *Elgar Companion to Marxist Economics*, edited by B. Fine and A. Saad Filho. Aldershot: Edward Elgar, 2009.

31. Fareel, Diana, Susan Lund, Eva Gerlemann, and Peter Seeburger, "The New Power Brokers: How Oil, Asia and Hedge Funds and Private Equity Are Shaping the Global Capital Markets," Mckinsey Global Institute, 2007.

32. Kenneth Rogoff and Carmen Reinhart, "Is the US Sub-Prime Market Crisis so Different?" *American Economic Review*, 98 (2, 2008): 339–44.

33. J. Darista and K. Erturk, "Reforming the International Monetary System," Background paper for World Economic and Social Survey, UN DESA, 2010.

34. K. Marx, *Capital: Volume III* (London: Penguin), 624.

35. R. Vasudevan, "From the Gold Standard to the Floating Dollar Standard."

36. R. Vasudevan, "Dollar Hegemony, Financialization and the Credit Crisis"; R. Vasudevan, "Credit Crisis."

CHAPTER 7

1. Institute of International Finance, Capital Flows to Emerging Market Economies. IIF Research Note, April 10, 2012.

2. Rainer Kattel, "Financial and Economic Crisis in Eastern Europe. International Development Economics Associates," 2010. http://www.networkideas.org/featart/jan2010/Eastern.Europe.pdf.

3. Kattel, "Financial and Economic Crisis in Eastern Europe."

4. IMF, *World Economic Outlook: Globalization and Inequality* (Washington DC, 2007).

5. Mary Stokes, "Eastern Europe: The Makings of a Cross Border Banking Nightmare," RGE Analysis, Roubini Global Economics, February, 2009. www.roubini.com.

6. F.M. Baldurrsson and R. Portes, "The Internationalization of Iceland's Financial Sector, "The Iceland Chamber of Commerce, 2007. http://www. iceland.org/media/jp/15921776Vid4WEB.pdf; W. Buiter and A. Sibert, "The Icelandic Banking Crisis and What to Do About It: The Lender of

Last Resort Theory of Optimal Currency Areas," *CEPR Policy Insight No. 26*, 2008.

7. A. Ward, "Iceland Accused of Negligence over Bank Crisis," *Financial Times*, April 13, 2010.

8. L. Story, L. Thomas, and N. Shwartz, "Wall Street Helped to Mask Debt Fuelling Europe's Crisis," *New York Times*, February 13, 2010.

9. Gustavo Piga, "Do Governments Use Financial Derivatives Appropriately? Evidence from Sovereign Borrowers in Developed Economies," *International Finance* 4 (2, 2001): 189–219.

10. Story, Thomas and Shwartz, "Wall Street Helped to Mask Debt Fuelling Europe's Crisis."

11. J. Rickard, "How Markets Attacked the Greek Piñata," *Financial Times*, February 11, 2010.

12. T. Barber, "EU Reluctantly Plans Athens Bailout," *Financial Times*, January 29, 2010.

13. W. Munchau, "Greece Can Expect no Gifts from Brussels," *Financial Times*, November 30, 2009.

14. K. Hope and M. Murphy. "Goldman Plays Key Role in Greece Rescue," *Financial Times*, January 28.

15. L. Thomas, "Patchwork Pension Plan Adds to Debt Woes," *New York Times*, March 11, 2010.

16. OECD, Factblog, Working 9-4.30, May 10, 2010.

17. OECD, Factblog, Keep on Working, February 11, 2010.

18. M. de Cecco, "The Crisis of the Export led Model in EU and its Consequences for European Integration Presented at the Institute for New Economic Thinking Conference at Cambridge," 2010. http://ineteconomics. org/sites/inet.civicactions.net/files/INET%20C%40K%20Paper%20Session%208%20-%20De%20Cecco.pdf.

19. C. Lapavitsas, A. Kaltenbrunner, D. Lindeo, J. Mitchell, J.P. Paincera, E. Pires, J. Powell, A. Stenfors and N. Teles, "Eurozone Crisis: Beggar Thyself and Thy Neighbor," *Research on Money and Finance*.

20. Kaltenbrunner Lapavitsas, Mitchell Lindeo, Pires Paincera, Stenfors and Teles, "Eurozone Crisis," 2010.

21. Lapavitsas, Kaltenbrunner, Lindeo, Mitchell, Paincera, Pires, Powell, Stenfors and Teles, "Eurozone Crisis."

22. M. Wolf, "The Eurozone Crisis Is Now a Greek Nightmare," *Financial Times*, March 10, 2010.

23. S. Danessku, J. Wilson and P. Jenkins, "Germany and France in Line of Fire," *Financial Times*, February 11, 2010; V. Fuhrman and S. Moffett, "Exposure to Greeks Weighs Heavily on German, French Banks," *Wall Street Journal*, February 10, 2010.

24. BIS Quarterly Review, June 2010.

25. J. Ewing, "Debt Burden Falls Heavily on Germany and France," *New York Times*, June 13, 2010.

26. N. Shwartz, "In and Out of Each Others European Wallets," *New York Times*, April 30, 2010.

27. K. Rogoff and C. Reinhardt, *This Time It Is Different: Eight Centuries of Financial folly* (Princeton: Princeton University Press, 2009).

28. M. Corkery, "What Is Wall Street's Exposure to Greece," *Wall Street Journal*, February 10, 2010.

29. A. Beattie, "A Reach Regained," *Financial Times*, April 22, 2010.

30. G. Tett, "Grim Echoes of Wall Street Crisis as Investors Face Mental Rubicon," *Financial Times*, May 6, 2010.

31. European Commission's Statistical Annex of the European Economy, Spring 2012. http://ec.europa.eu/economy_finance/publications/european_economy/2012/pdf/2012-05-11-stat-annex_en.pdf.

32. T. Johnson, "A Wider Radius," *Financial Times*, January 27, 2010.

33. J.C. de Swann, "China Goes to Wall Street: China's Evolving US Investment Strategy," *Foreign Affairs*, April 29.

34. P. Jenkins, "China Lenders Eclipse US Rivals," *Financial Times*, January 10.

35. R. Cookson, "Banks Back Switch to Renminbi Trade," *Financial Times*, August 26, 2010.

36. J. Kynge, "Central Plot of US China Ties Faces Off-Stage Challenge," *Financial Times*, January 8, 2010.

37. G. Dyer, "China Seeks to Ease Pace of Lending," *Financial Times*, February 13, 2010.

38. N. Roubini, "US-China Currency and Trade Collision Course."

39. D. Pilling, "The Dark Side of China's Dream," *Financial Times*, May 27, 2010; D. Barboza, "Deaths Shake a Titan in China," *New York Times*, May 27, 2010.

CHAPTER 8

1. E. Saez, "Striking It Richer," March 9, 2012. http://elsa.berkeley.edu/~saez/saez-UStopincomes-2010.pdf.

2. M. Friedman, *Capitalism and Freedom*, Preface (Chicago: University of Chicago Press, 1982).

3. N. Klein, *Shock Doctrine: The Rise of Disaster Capitalism* (New York: Picador, 2007).

4. Zhou Xiaochuan, "Reform the International Monetary System. Peoples Bank of China," 2009. http://www.pbc.gov.cn/english/detail.asp?col=6500&id=178.

5. United Nations, Recommendations by the Commission of Experts of the President of the General assembly on Reforms of the international Monetary System, 2009.

6. Institute of International Finance, "Capital Flows to Emerging Market Economies," Washington, 2012.

7. K. Bradsher and D. Barboza, "Strike in China Highlights Gap in Workers Pay," *New York Times*, May 29, 2010; H. Dongfan, "China's Workers Are Stirring," *New York Times*, June 17, 2010.

8. N. Fergusson, *Ascent of Money: A Financial History of the World* (New York: Penguin Press, 2008).

9. C. Reinhardt and K. Rogoff, *This Time It Is Different: 80 Years of Financial Folly* (Princeton University Press, 2009).

10. L. Story, "Banks Shared Clients Profits, but Not Losses," *New York Times*, October 17, 2010.

11. Matt Taibbibi, "The Scam Wall Street Learnt from the Mafia," *Rolling Stones*, July 5, 2012. http://www.rollingstone.com/politics/news/the-scam-wall-street-learned-from-the-mafia-20120620.

12. Taibbibi, "The Scam Wall Street Learnt from the Mafia."

13. Economist, "The LIBOR Scandal: The Rotten Heart of Finance," *Economist*, July 7, 2012.

14. M. Zuckerman, "America's Public Servants Are Now Its Masters," *Financial Times*, September 9, 2010; Wall Street Journal, "The Government Pay Boom," *Wall Street Journal*, March 26, 2010.

15. J. Bivens and H. Shierholz, "Three Years into Recovery, Just How much has State and Local Austerity Hurt Job Growth?" EPI blog, July 6, 2012. http://www.epi.org/blog/years-recovery-state-local-austerity-hurt/.

16. Editorial, "Governor Walkers Pretext," *New York Times*, February 17, 2011.

17. F. Rich, "Billionaires Bankrolling the Tea Party," *New York Times*, August 28, 2010.

18. J. Ashkenas, M. Ericson, A. Parlapiano, and D. Willis, "The 2012 Money Race: Compare the candidates," *New York Times*, September 30, 2012. http://elections.nytimes.com/2012/campaign-finance.

Some Suggestions for Further Reading

In writing this book I wanted to provide an accessible account of the structural roots and unfolding consequences of the current global crisis. My hope is that those interested in understanding these significant events would find this a useful point of entry to the vast literature on the crisis and its aftermath. For those whose appetite has been whetted, below are a few (highly selective) suggestions for further exploring some of the themes addressed in the book.

THE WORLD OF FINANCE

Y. Smith, demystifies the arcane world of finance with devastating clarity in *Econned: How unenlightened self interest undermined democracy and corrupted capitalism,* (Palgrave-Macmillan, New York, 2010). For a searing analysis of the role and function of financial markets read Doug Henwood's *Wall Street: How it works and for whom,* (Verso, London 1998). Gillian Tett's *Fools Gold: How the bold dream of a small tribe at J.P. Morgan was corrupted by Wall Street greed and unleashed a catastrophe* Free Press New York 2009 provides a lucid account of the instruments and players involved in the meltdown. D. Baker's, *Plunder and Blunder: The Rise and Fall of the Bubble economy*, Polipoint Press, 2009 chronicles the policy shifts since the 80's that boosted the growth of finance.

THE DOMINATION BY FINANCE OF THE POLICY RESPONSE

13 Bankers: The Wall Street takeover and the next financial meltdown, Pantheon Books, New York by Simon Johnson and James Kwaak is sharp critique of the power of the financial plutocracy. Other books exploring this theme are Gretta Krippner's *Capitalizing on Crisis: The Political Origins of the Rise of Finance*, Harvard University Press, Cambridge MA, 2012 and Naomi Prins's *It Takes a Pillage; An epic tale of power deceit and untold trillion*, Wiley, New Jersey, 2010. J. Stiglitz engages with the flawed policy regime that helped generate the meltdown and the missteps in the economic policy response in *Freefall: America, Free Markets and the sinking of the global economy*, W.W. Norton, New York, 2010. In *The New Lombard Street: How the Fed became a dealer of last resort*, Princeton University Press, Princeton 2011, Perry Mehrling explores the manner in which central bank policy adapted to the evolution of finance.

CLASS STRUCTURE AND THE CONTRADICTIONS OF CONTEMPORARY CAPITALISM

For an elaboration of the changing alignment of class forces and the rise to dominance of corporate and financial capital read Gerard Dumenil and Dominique Levy's *Capital Resurgent: Roots of Neoliberal Revolution*, Andrew Glyn's *Capital Unleashed:*

Finance, Globalization and Welfare, (Oxford University Press, USA, 2007), R. Brenner's, The Economics of Global Turbulence, (Verso, London 2006) and *The Boom and the Bubble* (Verso London, 2003). Gerard Dumenil and D. Levy, *The Crisis of Neoliberalism,* (Harvard University Press, 2010) is a magisterial and empirically rich exploration of the class origins of the current crisis. Among the other recent books on the structural roots of the crisis are G. Albo, L. Panitch and S. Gindin, *In and Out of Crisis: The Global Financial Meltdown and Left Alternatives,* (P.M. Press, 2010) J.B. Foster and F. Magdoff, *The Great Financial Crisis: Causes and Consequences,* (Monthly Review Press, New York, 2009); David Harvey, *The Enigma of Capital and the Crisis of Capitalism,* (Oxford University Press, London, 2010), David McNally, *Global Slump: The Economics and Politics of Crisis and Resistance* and Michael Hudson, *The Bubble and beyond: Fictitous Capital, Debt deflation and the Global Crisis,* (Islet, 2012). Socialist Register has two volumes devoted to the recent crisis: *Socialist Register 2011 The Crisis This Time* ((Monthly Review Press, New York, 2011) and *Socialist Register 2012: The Crisis and the Left* (Monthly Review Press, New York, 2011)

DOLLAR HEGEMONY AND THE GLOBAL RAMIFICATIONS OF THE CRISIS

Michael Hudson's *Super Imperialism: The Origin and Fundamentals of U.S. World Dominance* (Pluto Press, London, 2003) is a brilliant analysis of the role of financial diplomacy in US imperial hegemony. Leo Panitch and Sam Gindin's *Global Capitalism and American Empire* (Merlin Press, London, 2004) is a thoughtful exploration of how the structural power of the US state was deployed to forge contemporary global neoliberal capitalism. Raghuram Rajan *Fault Lines: How Hidden Fractures Still Threaten the World Economy* Princeton University Press (August 8, 2011) highlights the perils of a world overly dependent on the indebted American consumer to power global economic growth and stave off global downturns. K. Rogoff and C. Reinhardt, in *This time it is different: Eight Centuries of Financial folly*, Princeton University Press, Princeton, 2009 provide an exhaustive historical survey of the varieties of financial crises across the globe. Costas Lapavistas' *Crisis in the Eurozone,* Verso, London, 2012 investigates the causal roots and repercussions of the sequel of the subprime market collapse in the eurozone crisis.

My arguments linking dollar hegemony and financialization to the crisis have been previously elaborated in my articles: 'Dollar Hegemony, Financialization and the Credit Crisis', *Review of Radical Political Economics* 41,3, 2009; 'Finance Imperialism and the hegemony of the dollar', *Monthly Review,* April 2008, 'The Credit Crisis: Is the International role of the dollar at stake?' *Monthly Review*, April 2009 and 'The Global Meltdown: Financialisation, Dollar Hegemony and the Sub-prime Market Collapse', *Economic and Political Weekly* XLIV, 13, March 28, 2009. I investigated the historical parallels to the International Gold Standard under British empire in my articles: 'Borrower of Last Resort: International adjustment and Liquidityin historical perspective' *Journal of Economic issues,* 42(4) 2008 and 'From the Gold Standard to the Floating Dollar standard: An Appraisal in the light of Marx's Theory of money', *Review of Radical Political Economy,* 41(4) 2009. The argument about the vulnerability emerging markets in Eastern Europe was put forward in my article 'Reforming the International Financial System: Core and Periphery Issues and the Dollar Standard, *Eknomiaz*, 72(3), 2009.

Index

About the Author

Ramaa Vasudevan is an Associate Professor at the Department of Economics, Colorado State University. She earlier held a visiting position at Barnard College, Columbia University. Before embarking on a PhD on *Trade Finance and Uneven Development* at the New School of Social Research, she also taught for many years at PGDAV College at Delhi University.

While her earlier research in India studied the transformation of labor markets in the colonial agrarian economy (a case study of two districts in Eastern UP), she is now focused on exploring the political economy of money and finance. She has written numerous articles in various journals including the *Cambridge Journal of Economics, Review of Radical Political Economics, Monthly Review*, and *Economic and Political Weekly* and has contributed chapters in *Global Economic and Financial Crisis: Essays from Economic and Political Weekly and Globalization and Development: A Handbook of New Perspectives.*